William Worthington

An Impartial Enquiry Into the Case of the Gospel Demoniacks

with an appendix, consisting of an essay on Scripture Demonology

William Worthington

An Impartial Enquiry Into the Case of the Gospel Demoniacks
with an appendix, consisting of an essay on Scripture Demonology

ISBN/EAN: 9783337284688

Printed in Europe, USA, Canada, Australia, Japan

Cover: Foto ©Lupo / pixelio.de

More available books at **www.hansebooks.com**

AN
IMPARTIAL ENQUIRY
INTO THE CASE OF THE
GOSPEL DEMONIACKS.

AN IMPARTIAL ENQUIRY INTO The Case of the Gospel Demoniacks.

WITH AN APPENDIX,

CONSISTING OF

An Essay on Scripture Demonology.

By WILLIAM WORTHINGTON, D.D.

> Quemadmodum multa fieri non posse, priusquam facta sunt, judicantur: Ita multa quoque, quæ antiquitùs facta; quia nos ea non vidimus, neque ratione assequimur; ex iis esse, quæ fieri non potuerunt, judicamus. Quæ certe summa insipientia est.
> Plin. Hist. Nat. lib. vii. cap. 1.

LONDON:

Printed for J. F. and C. RIVINGTON, in St. Paul's Church-yard; T. PAYNE and Son, at the Meuse Gate; and B. WHITE, in Fleet-street.

MDCCLXXVII.

AN IMPARTIAL ENQUIRY

INTO THE CASE OF

THE GOSPEL DEMONIACKS.

DEMONIACAL poſſeſſions are ſo frequently mentioned in the goſpel; and make ſo conſiderable a part of it; and the miracles wrought with regard to them are ſo many, and ſo ſignal; and conſtitute ſo large a proportion in the evidence of ſcripture-miracles; that it is of great importance to the cauſe of Chriſtianity, to aſcertain the nature, both of the one, and the other; and to determine the controverſy concerning them with preciſion.

The queſtion is, Whether theſe poſſeſſions were real, or imaginary? And whether the miracles, wrought with regard to them, were

were real dispossessions of evil spirits out of the bodies of men? or were performed for the cure of some natural distempers, under that notion; in conformity with which, and the vulgar language concerning them, the distempers, and the cure of them, are described, as possessions, and dispossessions?

This is a question of facts. As such therefore it should be considered: And by reducing it to this point, and divesting it of all such considerations as are not necessarily connected with it, this question will be brought to a short issue.

Facts are objects of sense; than which there is nothing we are less liable to be deceived in. They are likewise the proper subjects of testimony. Testimony concerning facts of distant times, and places, is conveyed down by tradition and history. The more numerous the facts of the same kind and nature are, so attested and conveyed, the more they confirm and ascertain each other. The more competent, credible, and numerous, the witnesses of those facts are; the more they corroborate the evidence they give upon the whole; and the more they increase the sum of it.

The

The more circumstantially the facts are related, and the more they have of particular incidents interwoven with them; the more scope and compass is given, for weighing and comparing the several circumstances with the facts, and with each other—the more room there is given to judge and see how they all tally together.—The less probability likewise of deception there is; and the less room for suspicion of fraud, or apprehension of error; because it is more difficult to forge, or mistake facts, which are related with a number of concomitant circumstances, and other incidental facts connected with them, than to forge, or mistake, the naked facts themselves.

Facts, of which we have no *data* to judge by, but such as arise from testimony—which have nothing in them that implies a contradiction—that is contrary to any known laws of nature—or that can be pronounced impossible—The report of such facts must be received on the credit of their own evidence, properly attested.

Facts, which are not objects of sense, may notwithstanding be sufficiently attested and ascertained by their effects and circumstances; and by that means may become the proper subjects of our belief; as well as all other revealed truths; and many unrevealed ones likewise.

Facts, otherwise strange and incredible in themselves, are yet to be believed, if there be a sufficient weight of evidence to overcome the incredibility of them, and powers sufficient to effect them: There being many *phænomena* in nature, the reality of which is certain; but which notwithstanding would not have been believed to be true, on any evidence less than demonstration.

Important facts, of remote antiquity, attested by a sufficient number of credible eye-witnesses; recorded by a number of historians, of the same age; and the history of them making a part of, and being interwoven with, other historical narrations, of great importance likewise; all together making an entire whole; and this complete history being carefully preserved, and delivered down, in a great number of languages, and copies of each, without interruption, through all succeeding ages—such facts, thus attested, circumstanced, guarded, and safely conveyed down, must have all the requisite marks of historical credibility, which the nature of the thing will admit of;

and therefore all that can be demanded, or desired.

But moreover, If such facts stand upon the evidence of divine testimony—If they are recorded by inspired writers—they have then a sanction above all that is human; which we are not only awed to acquiesce in; but are invited to repose our trust and confidence in the truth and reality of them, with a full assurance of faith.

Let us now examine the narrations, which we meet with in the gospels, of persons possessed with evil spirits, and dispossessed of them, by these *criteria*.

This enquiry will consist:

I. Of an examination into those facts themselves, together with their circumstances.

II. Into the competency of the witnesses: And

III. Into the sufficiency of the evidence.

Throughout the whole will be intersperfed remarks on what hath been advanced in opposition to the reality of these facts. To that will be added such observations as arise from the subject; together with an Appendix by way of Essay on Scripture Demonology.

I. And here it is, in the first place, to be observed, That these narrations have all the appearance of narrations of facts—That they run in the usual style of history, as other historical facts are generally related—That there is not the least intimation given anywhere, throughout the Scriptures, that they are to be understood otherwise, than as real matters of fact. Neither would any man, of a plain understanding, than which nothing more is requisite to judge of facts, entertain the least doubt of their reality; taking them, as he finds them in his bible; without knowing any thing of the disputes raised about them: Which affords good grounds of presumption, that they are facts accordingly.

Matters of doctrine are delivered in the gospels, as doctrine. Precepts of morality, as such. Parables are prefaced, and related, as parables. Prophecies are recited in the prophetical language: And matters of fact are, all alike, reported as facts, that really happened; and are generally received, as such.

The facts under consideration are related indifferently, as they arise; often among other facts; in the same style and manner

manner with them. Nor can it well be conceived, how they could be recorded, as facts, in a more simple, or authentick manner.

Let us come to a nearer view of them. Some of these facts are mentioned in general terms. Others are particularly and circumstantially related. The general accounts of possessions and dispossessions occur so often in the gospels, that they constitute a great notoriety. As we meet with them frequently, we likewise find a very distinct account of them. Sometimes they appear separately by themselves; and though at other times they stand in connection with other facts; and those who are possessed with devils, are mentioned among such as labour under other complaints; yet they are sufficiently distinguished from them: Neither is there room for confounding or mistaking the one, for the other.

Thus, in the first account of this matter, which we have in the gospel, it is said, *That they brought unto Jesus all sick people, that were taken with diverse diseases, and torments; and those which were possessed with devils; and those which were lunatick; and* *those that had the palsy*; and he healed them [*]. Where we may observe, that those which were possessed with devils are distinguished from all such as laboured under any other complaints, both before, and after; and particularly from *those that were taken with torments*, mentioned next before; and *those that were lunatick*, next after: Whence it appears, that all kinds of torments are not ascribed to, nor described by, possessions; though possession was the cause of many; and that all lunatick persons are not described, nor rendered such by having evil spirits, though, I doubt not, many were. Those therefore, among other common diseases, are to be ascribed to natural causes.

It is asserted and maintained, " that the " demoniacks spoken of in the New Testa- " ment, were all either mad-men, or epi- " lepticks [†]." Epilepticks and lunaticks are reckoned the same, under different names, as the paroxysms of epilepsy are often observed to come on at the change of the moon: But the demoniacks in the place before us, were not lunaticks, or epilep-

[*] Matt. iv. 24.
[†] Essay on the Demoniacks of the New Testament, p. 92.

ticks

ticks; becaufe thofe *that were poffeffed with devils*, and *thofe which were lunaticks*, are diftinctly mentioned; as perfons labouring under different diforders: Nor doth it appear, that thefe demoniacks had any natural diforder at all.

And we fhall hereafter find demoniacks mentioned without reference to any diftemper whatfoever. And, I believe, I may challenge any one to point out the place, where it is exprefsly faid, or whence it may be fairly inferred, That demoniacks, or any one demoniack, had any other madnefs, or epilepfy, or other complaint, than fuch as appears to have been actually caufed by the poffeffion, with which they were feized. They are defcribed in language peculiar to their cafe; and a particular ftyle and phrafeology is obferved with regard to them. *Heal the fick; cleanfe the lepers; raife the dead*; caft out devils*. This was the term generally made ufe of in this refpect. —A term very proper for the purpofe. But of what difeafe could it be properly ufed, where there was no devil to be caft out?

Madneffes and epilepfies are never faid to be caft out. In a word, I cannot find, that

---

* Matt. x. 8.

those, who were possessed with devils, had any other complaint, but what was caused or attended by the possession; and this alone undoubtedly was more than sufficient.

When our Saviour was warned by the Pharisees of Herod's intent to kill him, *Go ye,* says he, *and tell that fox, Behold I cast out devils, and I do cures to-day, and to-morrow; and the third day I shall be perfected**. Can it be conceived, that this message was capable of being understood otherwise than in the plain literal sense of the words? Or, that the terms were ambiguous, and admitted of two senses? One of which must be false; which therefore so crafty and subtile a man would not fail to interpret them in, and expose Christ as a false pretender.

Behold, says he, *I cast out devils!* He singles out this from among his other miraculous cures, and bespeaks the attention of this wicked prince to it, as the most beneficial to his subjects, of all the good works, for which, it seems, he meditated our blessed Lord's destruction.

* Luke xiii. 32.

There are many other general accounts of our Saviour's casting out devils*. The time for working these, and his other salutary miracles, was often in the evening. *When even was come, they brought unto him many that were possessed with devils, and he cast out the spirits with his word* †. When the labour of the day was over, the people had most leisure for bringing those who wanted relief from their several maladies to the divine physician. And hence, by the way, as well as from several other places in scripture, it appears, that the *Jews* were an industrious set of people, and good husbands of their time.

Our Lord did not only eject devils himself; but he delegated the same power to others—to the twelve ‡; to the seventy disciples §; and even indiscriminately to believers in general ‖. Than which there cannot be a more convincing proof of his divine power and absolute dominion over

---

* Mark i. 39—iii. 11. Luke vi. 18.—vii. 21.—viii. 2.
† Matt. viii. 16. Comp. Mark i. 32. 34. Luke iv. 40, 41.
‡ Matt. x. 1—8. Mark iii. 15.—vi. 13. Luke ix. 1. Acts v. 16.—viii. 8.
§ Luke x. 17.
‖ Mark xvi. 17.

evil

evil spirits. His commission and promise, in this respect, is so full and absolute; and the success of his disciples, in the execution of it, was such, that they mutually corroborate each other. It is well known, particularly from the frequent appeals, which the christian Apologists make to it, that this power continued in the church for some ages; and was exercised with such success, that at length it became in a manner needless, when there were left scarce any objects of it in christian countries; and then no wonder it ceased. It appears, that simple and illiterate christians ejected devils, by invoking the name of Jesus, so low down as the middle of the third century *.

Thus stand the general accounts of possessions and dispossessions in the gospel, most, if not all, of which I have taken notice of. And these are expressed in terms, so plain and clear, so pertinent and proper, that it would be difficult to find words that would be more significant.

There is nothing ambiguous, or doubtful in them, which can afford the least ground to suspect, that the possessions were not real;

* Ἰδιῶται τὸ τοιοῦτον πράττουσι. Origen. contra Celf. lib. vii. p. 334.

the Case of the Gospel Demoniacks. 13

or that the dispossessions were not really and truly effected: And whether they are taken in their separate, or collective capacity; whether, as standing each by itself, or as mixt with other relations; we cannot find the least room given by them, for supposing, according to any known rules of good writing, that all, or any of these possessions were only imaginary, or that they had no other existence, than a fanciful one. Point out any single word, that looks that way—that betrays any doubtful, or equivocal meaning; that is capable of such an interpretation; or that can, by any force of criticism, be tortured into such a sense; or else suffer the simple literal meaning to remain undisturbed.

Perhaps it may be thought, that a general view of things only lets us into a general and superficial acquaintance with them: But when we meet with particular and circumstantial relations of them, we have opportunities of inspecting and scrutinizing them more narrowly and minutely; and of discussing them more thoroughly; whereby we obtain a more intimate and perfect knowledge of them.

Great

Great is truth, and more precious than all things; and the opinion, or doctrine, that will not bear the test of truth; be it ever so venerable for age or authority; ought to be sacrificed to it.

Let us therefore descend to accounts of particular possessions; and examine them, as with candour, so with severity; in order to find out the true and genuine nature of them; for the discovery of which, some new light may, now and then, be perhaps struck out from this enquiry.

I. The first particular account of a demoniack, which we meet with in the gospel, is that of a man, in the synagogue of *Capernaum*, with an unclean spirit *. St. *Luke* calls him *a spirit of an unclean devil* †: Which is much stronger, by using two different names, in construction with each other, for the same wicked Being; and thus more cogently evincing the reality of the possession. And to put it beyond all doubt, *the Spirit cried out with a loud voice, saying, Let us alone: What have we to do with thee, thou Jesus of Nazareth? Art thou come to destroy us? I know thee, who*

---

* Mark i. 23.
† Luke iv. 33. This expression, *The spirits of devils*, is used Rev. xvi. 14.

thou

thou art, the holy one of God. Now that it was the evil fpirit in the man, and not the man himfelf, and without any evil fpirit, that cried, and prayed, and expoftulated with Chrift, and made this confeffion to him, appears from his fpeaking in the plural number; either in the name of the man, and himfelf; or rather in his own name, and that of his fraternity of evil fpirits. This appears more plainly ftill, from our Saviour's directing his difcourfe to him, rebuking him, and faying, *Hold thy peace, and come out of him.*

It will perhaps be pleaded, That the man only fancied himfelf to be poffeffed; when he talked, and raved, and perfonated the devil in this manner. But will it not then be neceffary to fuppofe likewife, that our Saviour fancied the fame thing; or at leaft that he humoured the poor crazy man, and confirmed him in his opinion, which made him fo very unhappy? Can this be fuppofed? Can it be fuppofed too, that our Lord would addrefs the man's diftemper, as a real perfon? Would he fuppofe his madnefs to articulate, and talk in this manner? Would he filence it, and order it to come out of the man? Surely there never was fo

bold

bold and improper a figure as this used in any language, or on any occasion.

But it doth not appear, that the man was in the least disordered in his senses. Neither of the evangelists mention any such thing; not even, as the effect of his possession. All that St. *Mark* says is, *That the Spirit tare him* *, *as he came out of him*; which would have been an odd description of a distemper. But this was not attended with any ill consequences, which probably were prevented by our Saviour: For St. *Luke* says, that the devil only *threw him down, when he came out of him, and hurt him not.*

But if there was here no superior intelligence, how came this man to be so knowing of himself? Whence had he his information concerning the divine nature of Christ; and of the work he was about, for the destruction of *Satan* and his kingdom? He was at that time but just entering on his ministry; and had but begun to preach in the synagogues of *Galilee.* He had scarce

---

* Some translate, *convulsed him,* as the Gr. σπαραξαν may very well be translated, and which better agrees with St. *Luke.* See Bp. *Pearce's* note on the place.

called

called half his twelve disciples*. And it doth not appear, that any but the *Baptist*, and those few, knew him to be the *Messiah*. How came this man to know him so well, who had no call, nor any information concerning him; as those disciples had? It is not probable they themselves could as yet know explicitly, that he was come to destroy their spiritual enemies. Whence could this madman, as he is supposed to have been, have that superior knowledge? It is unconceivable, that the mere man, out of his senses, or in them, could have had so much divine knowledge.

But the evil spirit, who possessed him, knew all this to his cost. It is but in the beginning of this chapter of St. *Luke*, that we are informed of Christ's temptation by the devil. As he knew, or apprehended, that Christ was sent to suppress him, and to destroy his kingdom; he was resolved to be beforehand with him, and to have the advantage of the first onset. He therefore boldly assaulted him; and persevered in carrying on the assault incessantly for forty days together. This gave him an opportunity

---

* Compare Matt. iv. 18. 22. Mark i. 16—20. And John i. 35. et seqq.

tunity of knowing *Jesus*, his office, and his power. He was conscious likewise of the provocation, which he had so lately given him to exercise his power over him. It was therefore very natural for him to cry out, as he loudly did, and to crave his mercy and forbearance. *Let us alone. What have we to do with thee, thou Jesus of Nazareth? Art thou come to destroy us? I know thee who thou art, the Holy one of God.*

What is there in this account that is forced, or unnatural? This great miracle carries its own evidence with it, and compels conviction. The whole congregation was *amazed, and questioned among themselves, saying, What a thing is this? What new doctrine is this?* that is enforced with such power and authority, that he *commandeth even the unclean spirits, and they do obey him?* The presence of an unclean spirit is here so manifest; and the contrary interpretation, when applied to this miracle, implies such improbability; that there seems not to be the least room left to doubt, which side of the question to take.

II. Of all the demoniacal possessions recorded in the New Testament, none is so much objected against—none with so much
freedom

freedom and boldness, as that of the *Gadarene* demoniack. How justly, will appear from a candid examination of the case, on a fair state of it; upon which alone I wish to rest it.

St. *Matthew* mentions two men possessed with devils *. *Mark* and *Luke* take notice but of one †; as being probably the most outrageous. In the first place we are told, that immediately upon our Saviour's landing on the coast, there met him out of the tombs a man with an unclean spirit; where having grown quite wild, and unmanageable, he always abode, night and day, crying, and cutting himself with stones. But this man, when he saw Jesus *afar* off, *immediately ran, and worshipped him*. A great change of behaviour this, in such a man! The least that it implies was some particular acquaintance the man must have had with the person of *Jesus*; it being an old observation, that friends and enemies are known at a distance. But what acquaintance could this man have had with him? A man, who had long fled from the con-

---

* Matt. viii. 28.
† Mark v. 1. Luke viii. 26.

verse of men, having *had devils a long time* *, whom other men could not approach with safety—who had always lived in desolate places, and in a country our Saviour had never before been in. There doth not seem the least probability that this man could have had any knowledge of *Jesus*; much less that he should know him to be the Son of God; and as such worship him; when as yet his own disciples had scarce arrived at such a degree of knowledge concerning him.

I do not really know how to account for this matter otherwise, than upon the same principles, on which the former case was solved; that this man was really and actually possessed by the devil; as he is said to have been. The devil was a being of superior intelligence; and had a particular opportunity of being well acquainted with *Jesus*; as hath been just now observed †. Hence it was, that he impelled the man to run and worship him; with intent, I apprehend, by this act of adoration and homage, to flatter him into some indulgence towards him.

* Luke viii. 27.
† P. 17.

But.

But *Jesus* knew *him* likewise, notwithstanding that he concealed himself in the body of the man. But instead of giving him any countenance, he instantly commanded him to quit possession. *Come out of the man, thou unclean spirit.* Upon this he appears to have been much distressed and disconcerted; and, crying with a loud voice, said, *What have I to do with thee, Jesus, thou son of the most high God?* I deny this to be disclaiming his authority *. It is evading it, if you please, had he known how. This language, we have seen, was used by the devil towards Christ, on a former occasion: And it may be illustrated from a passage in the Old Testament; where the same form of speech is used, without any disrespectful meaning.

What have I to do with thee, thou king of Judah? I come not against thee this day; but against the house wherewith I have war, said *Necho* king of Egypt to *Josiah* †. *What have I to do with thee, Jesus, thou son of the most high God?* said *Satan* to *Christ.* I do not presume to contend with thee; or to offer any indignity to thy person. All his aim

---

* See Essay on demoniacks, p. 262.
† 2 Chron. xxxv. 21.

was,

was, to plague and torment ordinary mortals. He knew it was to no purpose to make any attempts upon the Saviour of the world; having been so lately foiled and baffled by him. He now was fully convinced of his superior power, *I adjure thee, by God*; I beg for God's sake, *that thou torment me not*. It seems to have been some relaxation and relief to these accursed spirits, to exchange their infernal prisons for the bodies of men; and to be permitted to shelter themselves in them from the divine vengeance. It at least afforded them the malicious pleasure of making whom they possessed partakers of their torments; and thereby alleviating them, in some measure, by having others to become sharers in them.

St. *Matthew* relates, that the devils asked Christ, *A*[,]*t thou come hither to torment us, before the time**? What time is this that is here referred to? Some think it to be the general judgement; when they were to receive their final sentence; and to be consigned to their eternal prisons; supposed to

---

* Matt. viii. 29.

be the deep, or abyfs, which they befought Chrift not to fend them into.

But I am rather inclined to think, that the time they meant was; when Chrift was to take poffeffion of his kingdom; and their own to be deftroyed; which they apprehended to be approaching; but which they hoped was not to come yet-a-while; as they hitherto faw no great appearances of it.

But it was not for them to know the times and the feafons. The kingdom of God cometh not with obfervation. It made its approaches by degrees, for the gradual difplay of his glory in this refpect.

After having ejected many devils himfelf, Chrift delegated this power, firft to his twelve apoftles*; and then to the feventy difciples †; who, when they returned with a joyful account of their fuccefs, *Lord, even the devils are fubject to us, through thy name*—Our Saviour takes occafion to fay, *I beheld Satan, as lightning, fall from heaven.* To which he adds, *Behold I give you power to tread on ferpents and fcorpions, and over all the power of the enemy* ‡. This fignifies the downfall

---

* Luke ix. 1.
† Ibid. x. 1.
‡ Ibid. x. 17, 18, 19.

of *Satan*'s kingdom, which by this time was in a great measure accomplished.

Hence our Saviour *in that time rejoiced in spirit*, and declared, *that all things were delivered to him of his Father* *. And as his own kingdom was to be erected on the ruins of that of *Satan*, he commissioned the seventy to preach, *That the kingdom of God was come nigh* †. And in allusion to this, our Saviour elsewhere declares, *Now is the judgment of this world: Now shall the prince of this world be cast out* ‡—cast out of his kingdom; as he, and his accursed associates, were at this time every day cast out of the bodies of men. This, therefore, I apprehend, was the time alluded to by the devils, when they asked Jesus, *Art thou come hither to torment us before the time?*

What is most remarkable in this case, and most ridiculed, is the *legion* of devils, mentioned in it, which next demands our attention. This is singled out to be laughed at, above all that is elsewhere said of de-

---

* Luke x. 21, 22.

† Ibid. x. 9. Compare Matt. iii. 2. iv. 17. Luke xxi. 31.

‡ Jo. xii. 31. St. *John* seldom takes notice of demoniacks. However, he uses the same form of speech in this respect with the other evangelists.

moniacal

moniacal poffeffions *. But, before we join in the outcry, let us fee whether any fatisfactory account can be given of this paffage, according to the literal fenfe; and what can be faid in fupport of it.

A very extraordiftary account, and as extraordinary a revelation, this concerning the *legion* certainly is, if it really be one: And, as fuch, the intent of the divine wifdom in making it feems to have been this; which cannot, by any ferious Chriftian, be thought unworthy of it.

To apprize mankind of the number of their fpiritual enemies—to fetch a confeffion out of their own mouths of this; and likewife to fhew how dreadfully they were combined againft the fons of men,—and in what multitudes they could unite, and, as it were, incorporate themfelves, even within the body of one poor mortal;—and, at the fame time, to manifeft his own power over them all, though ever fo numerous, and ever fo formidably muftered together; our Saviour takes the opportunity of afking the devil his name; as we find feveral of them mentioned by name in the Scripture.

* See note from *Rouffeau*, in the Effay on Demoniacks, p. 4. and p. 260. ibid.

To this the infernal spirit anfwered, that his name was *Legion*. *For, as he adds, we are many.* Such a number of them being collected together, feems, as if they meant to make head againft the Captain of our Salvation. The Devil found, that himfelf alone was not a match for him, and he faw with what eafe he expelled the evil fpirits fingly out of men's bodies. Therefore, before he would give up the conteft, he was refolved to try what numbers might do; and whether fuch a formidable hoft would not intimidate him from the attempt to difpoffefs them all together; and whether they could not keep poffeffion of this one man in fpite of him.

But in vain: A legion was but a poor force to withftand him, who, upon occafion, had no lefs than twelve legions of holy angels at his command. The daftardly crew, therefore, defpairing, that their numbers would be any protection to them, and fearing to provoke him, whofe power they dreaded; inftantly, and in the fame breath, as it were, fell to praying. *They befought him much, that he would not fend them out of the country* *: Which feems to have

* Mark v. 10.

been

been a very wicked one, and therefore the fitter for their abode; some proof of which will seen hereafter. Or, if he would not grant them this petition, *they besought him*, that of all things, *he would not command them to go into the deep* *. The general opinion is, That, by the deep, or abyss, is here to be understood the bottomless pit of hell; whither the devils, above all things, dreaded to be sent; as it was to be the place of their final doom. But I am rather inclined to think, that, by the deep here, they meant the sea, or lake of *Gennesareth* adjoining; into which they had some apprehensions of being sentenced. This would be ridding the country of them; and their being there imprisoned, without having any men's bodies to enter, that would be some punishment and mortification to them. But whether it was to an eternal, or a temporary prison, that these evil spirits feared to be sent; rather than to be doomed to either, they were willing to take up with the bodies of the most filthy animals. Therefore they beseech our Lord,—*If thou cast us out*,—as he had before commanded the unclean spirit to come out of the man.—If thou art resolved upon casting us out, *suffer us to go*

---

* Luke viii. 31.

away

away into the herd of swine; which was feeding at some distance, on the neighbouring mountain. Those unclean beasts were fit receptacles for these unclean spirits: Therefore our Saviour readily granted their request; and, as such, needed not to command their putting it in execution, as he is represented to have done*. St. *Matthew's* words are, *Suffer us to go away into the herd of swine. And he said unto them, Go:* Which word, as it refers to the request, surely implies no more than permission. St. *Mark's* words are, *All the devils besought him, saying, Send us into the swine, that we may enter into them. And forthwith Jesus gave them leave.* St. *Luke,* in like manner, says, *They besought him, that he would suffer them to enter into the swine: And he suffered them. Then went the devils out of the man, and entered into the swine* †. Since they were not permitted to do greater mischief; they were content to do less, rather than to be deprived of the power of doing

---

* Essay on Demoniacks, p. 300.

† Ejicere diabolum ex homine, Christi fuit actio; in porcos, ut irent, nullâ actione Christi erat opus: hoc enim optabant ipsi diaboli; et viribus nativis id ipsum efficere poterant, dum ne vi majore impedirentur. Non ergo Christus in hâc re vim agentem exeruit; sed vim impedire valentem sustinuit. Grot. in Matt. viii. 31.

any at all. As they were no longer suffered to annoy men's persons, it was some gratification to their malice to injure men in their properties.

The devils, no doubt, had a farther view in their request to enter into the swine; which was to incense the owners against our Saviour for their loss of them, which would be imputed to him; and the people of the country in general, for fear of the like damage being done to them, were uneasy at his stay among them, and therefore *prayed him to depart out of their coasts.*

By this means, the devils likewise counteracted, and hoped to defeat the good effects of this miracle upon the man, in the conversion of the people; by prejudicing them against the author of it, for the loss of the swine. They were notwithstanding baffled and frustrated in all their subtil contrivances. They made two requests to our Saviour, which were both granted; and yet brought on the evil they deprecated, and plunged them into the abyss they hoped to avoid by them. Being suffered to enter the swine, which they prayed for, they were precipitated into the deep, which they prayed against. For, I take it, that the drowning of the swine was contrary to the intentions

intentions of the unclean spirits *; to whom it is not ascribed; but that it proceeded from the rage, which the possession naturally produced in them; the effect and consequence of which [the devils were restrained from controuling, or putting a stop to. So that they were caught in their own snare, and worked their own overthrow.

The inhabitants of this country seem to have been an impious people; and as they were averse to our Saviour's continuance among them; so being unworthy of his presence, he withdrew. The owners of the swine particularly were justly punished by the loss of them, for feeding creatures to be a snare to the Jews; the use of which they were forbidden by their law. And if they were Jews themselves, they were punished still more deservedly.

Our Saviour, notwithstanding, was not defeated in the intent of the miracle. He left a special preacher, to proclaim the truth and benefit of it; even the man himself on whom it was wrought. He was desirous of accompanying his deliverer, and continuing with him; in order, probably, to

---

* See Essay on Demoniacks, p. 265.

be under his protection from the evil spirits, should they return to molest him; as well as to become his disciple. But our Lord ordered him to stay in the country; where he would henceforth be in no danger; and where he would be more useful likewise, in making God's mercies to him more generally known. And he failed not *to publish, through the whole city, and all Decapolis, what great things Jesus had done for him,* to the astonishment of all; and, without doubt, to the conversion of many.

St. *Chrysostom,* who never dreamed of any thing unreal in this case, assigns many reasons for our Saviour's permitting the devils to enter the swine, the substance of which chiefly is, " To teach mankind how
" great the malignity of these wicked ty-
" rants," as he calls them, " is; who are
" perpetually lying in wait to destroy—un-
" der what restraints they providentially
" are; insomuch, that they cannot enter
" even the bodies of swine, without the di-
" vine permission; — that, as they have a
" greater hatred towards men, than brutes,
" they would precipitate them into the like
" destruction with that of the swine; if
" they were not over-ruled by the divine
" pro-

" providence: — and that Chrift's farther
" intention in this miracle was, to mani-
" feft his own power over thofe malignant
" fpirits*."

Upon the whole, I do not fee, in this narrative, any thing, which, in its hiftorical and literal fenfe, to a candid and unprejudced mind, is inconfiftent with itfelf; or unfuitable to the feveral characters that appear in it; much lefs do I fee any thing that deferves to be treated with contempt and ridicule.

The affrighted fwine-herds were heralds of the fact; and the whole city and country of the *Gadarenes*, round about, ran together to become witneffes of it. Every circumftance concurs to eftablifh the notoriety as well as reality of the incident; and the finger of God is manifeft throughout the whole.

It not only exhibits a moft remarkable difplay of the divine power; but fpecial characters of divine wifdom likewife are to be traced in it. And it opens fuch difcoveries into the world of fpirits, as are not to be met with elfewhere in holy writ.

---

* S. Chryfoft. Hom. in Matth. xxviii. tom. ii. p. 197.

Let us now examine the case of the *Gadarene* demoniack, on the supposition of his being a mere madman, and that his possession was no more than an imaginary one. This account hath one advantage; that there is nothing so extravagant, that a person deprived of his reason may not be supposed, by the force of a wild and disordered imagination, to fancy to himself; which is an easy way of accounting for any thing, even the greatest absurdities. There are, notwithstanding, in the present case, many things that cannot be accounted for on this hypothesis, with any degree of probability.

It hath been already observed, how improbable it is, that this man, of himself, could, in his condition, and under all the circumstances of his case, have the least knowledge of *Jesus*; much less probable is it, that he should have such an intimate knowledge of him, as he is represented to have had, than which the highest intelligences could not have a greater.

This man appears to have been possessed with strength more than human; for it plainly surpassed all human powers and means to subdue. Search *Bedlam*, and enquire of all the faculty there, whether they ever knew,

knew, or heard of a mere madman, that could be paralleled with this?

His fancied poffeffion is acknowledged to have been owing to a notion, which had long obtained in the world, that there were fuch things as real poffeffions; and which he might have heard of. But if there never had been any fuch things as real poffeffions at all, how will you account for thofe notions?

It is faid, that the doctrine of poffeffions, be it true or falfe, was not originally founded on revelation*. What was it then founded upon? All error fuppofes truth, which it is a deviation from; and all counterfeits muft have realities before them to mimick and copy from. There may be, and I doubt not there have been, many counterfeit poffeffions: But there never would have been one in the world, nor would any fuch thing ever have been thought of, if there never had been any real poffeffions; which they were meant to pafs for. And, as there could not be any other ground for counterfeit poffeffions than real ones: fo neither could

---

* Effay on Demoniacks, p. 173. The contrary to this affertion will be fhewn hereafter.

the

the notion of possessions in general have sprung from any other source than that of reality: Whence the truth and justness of that notion necessarily follows.

But if this madman might have heard of possessions, is it likely, he would ever have heard of legions of devils, crowding themselves into the body of one man? A man must have as strong an imagination as he, to believe this. There are other difficulties to encounter on this hypothesis.

Can the madness and destruction of the swine be accounted for from the fancy or madness of the man? He is indeed acknowledged to have been restored to his right mind, before this happened. But could a man or two, in or out of their senses, force two thousand of such perverse animals, in spite of their keepers, headlong into the sea*? This indeed is given up. Was the madness then catching? Were the swine infected with the same fancy of being possessed?

And would it operate upon them in still a more fatal manner? They were feeding quietly on the mountain the minute before.

* See Essay on Demoniacks, p. 280.

If they were not poffeffed with the devils, what did poffefs them, thus inftantly to rufh upon their deftruction?

I have a right to afk thefe queftions; becaufe, if you adopt a general principle for folving all difficulties, you muft carry it throughout: But, if you drop it in one part, and only make a partial ufe of it, when it is convenient, the chain is broken, and the ftory hangs but ill together.

To refolve the cataftrophe of the fwine into the divine agency*, is quitting that principle, and having recourfe to another. The madnefs of the man was feen to be foreign, and inadequate to the purpofe: Therefore that is dropt, and a general principle is adopted, which is adequate to every purpofe, and contains an anfwer to any queftion. The divine power undoubtedly might drive the fwine mad, and precipitate them into the fea: And fo it might have driven the man mad; as his madnefs, or poffeffion, call it what you will, was not without the divine permiffion. But for the divine power to exert itfelf for this purpofe, at that inftant of time, when it is faid the devils went out

---

* See Effay on Demoniacks, p. 293.

of the man, and went into the swine, what motive could the divine wisdom have for this? Was this to correct the false notions of the world concerning the power of demons? Would it not, on the contrary, be the most effectual means of confirming them?

St. *Chrysostom* draws an argument from the destruction of the swine, to prove, that the whole of this account was that of real facts, and not a scenical representation*.

I wish it were considered, what little regard is paid to the inspired penmen of this narrative, by those who put this sense upon it. *Rousseau* scoffs at their account of the *legion*, with much disdain: And a preacher of the gospel adopts the raillery of this unbeliever, and treats them no less disrespectfully.

St. *Mark* relates, that the unclean spirit said, *my name is legion; for we are many* †. These, in their account, are the man's own words: For they will not allow, he had, in

---

* Ἵνα μη τις σκηνην ειναι νομιση τα γενομενα, αλλα πιστευ- ση σαφως, ὁτι εξηλθεν ὁ δαιμων· απο τε θανάτε των χοιρων τέτο γινέται καταδηλον. Chrysost. ib. p. 198.

† Mark v. 9.

reality, any unclean spirit: To which therefore it may be said in answer, that he had a lying spirit, if he had none other. For on this supposition he belied himself. But to give no handle for cavilling at his, or the devil's testimony, the evangelist afterwards mentions him, on his own testimony, as having had the legion*; though no more regard is paid to the one, than to the other. And St. *Luke* yet more directly relates, as his own testimony, that when *Jesus* asked him his name, he said, *Legion* ; *because*, says the evangelist, *many devils were entered into him* †. Where we see, that the divine writer positively asserts, *that many devils were entered into the man*. The author of the Essay, on the contrary, pertinaciously contends, that there had not so much as one devil entered into him. Here is a downright, and palpable contradiction. I leave him to his own reflections upon it.

I should be glad to know, how the several evangelists could express themselves with more clearness and precision, concerning this matter, if they meant to write

---

* Mark v. 15.
† Luke viii. 30.

true history; and did not conspire to deceive the world, throughout all ages, ever since.

But, above all, how is the veneration, that is due to the Son of God, secured, on this hypothesis? Doth it represent his conduct, in a manner suitable to his divine character? Did it become him to hold a conversation with a mad-man? And even with his very distemper, ascribing a personality to the madness itself? Would he flatter the poor man's insanity? Would he confirm him in it? Would he act a feigned part;—keep up the conversation, and tempt him with a question, that, in this view, was certainly a very idle one, and of no use, but to bespeak a most wild and extravagant answer — which could serve no other purpose, than to beget, or countenance, in men, a superstitious opinion " of millions of spiritual " creatures walking the earth unseen," if there were in reality none such? Would not the divine physician rather have cured the poor man, of his distemper, if it was no more than common madness, as he did thousands of others, by a word's speaking? Nor surely would he have been wanting on such an occasion, to drop a hint at least, that might contribute to the cure of the superstitious notion of demoniacal possessions, if it was such, in all the by-standers, as well as in the man himself?

"The miracle performed upon the "swine, we are told, was calculated to cor- "rect the false notions concerning the "power of demons *:" But we are not told how it answered this end. It was certainly a very preposterous way of eradicating notions that were "so deeply rooted in the "minds of men." Many commentators are of opinion that it confirms these notions more than any of the other miracles of this kind; and all unprejudiced persons must concur with them.

And I should be glad to know, by what means, in what words, and by what actions, our blessed Lord could have established these notions more effectually. Above all things, why did our Saviour use "the sovereign word "Go †;" Why did he expressly send, and even command, the unclean spirits, since you will have it to have been so, to go into the swine ‡? Had he no meaning in this?

* Essay on Demoniacks, p. 299.
† Ibid. p. 301.
‡ Ibid. p. 293.

Did

Did he indeed mean the direct contrary? He meant undoubtedly, to demonstrate the existence of these evil spirits, together with the immense number of them. He meant, in this peculiar manner, by which the evil spirits went out of the man, and entered into the swine, to convince all that are not hardened against conviction, that this could not proceed from inert matter; but that these must have been active intelligent beings endowed with this loco-motive power. And as it was pride that cast these accursed spirits out of heaven, he went farther, by this special debasement of them, to mortify this inveterate pride of their nature, than they had ever suffered before.

In a word, if you say there were no devils here; you may as well say, there were no swine.

Before I quitt this case, I would observe, that I cannot discover any insanity in either of these demoniacks; but what, in the language of the faculty, was symptomatical; and solely effected by the devils that possessed them. The first thing said of them by St. *Matthew* is, *that there met Jesus,* not two madmen, but *two men possessed with devils.*

vils *. St. *Mark* prefaces his account with saying, that *there immediately met him out of the tombs a man with an unclean spirit* †. Luke says, *he had devils a long time* ‡. Then follow, in all the three, their several accounts of the disorder, with all the violent paroxysms of it; which therefore is naturally to be attributed to the possession, as the forementioned cause of it. Hence all their outrages against themselves and others. And hence it is said of the principal of them, that as soon as the devils had been cast out of him, the man came to himself; and was seen *sitting at the feet of Jesus, cloathed, and in his right mind.* The cause being removed, the effect ceased of course. And it remains to be proved, that any of the gospel-demoniacks were originally maniacks; and that their insanity, or the other diseases under which they laboured, proceeded merely from natural causes.

It is farther to be observed; that this demoniack was driven by the devil into the wilderness §. This is in character. The

---

* Matt. viii. 28.
† Mark v. 2.
‡ Luke viii. 27.
§ Ibid. viii. 29.

wilderness

wilderness was the place into which he drave Christ *; and in which, for the privacy of it, he chose to conflict with him. The man's constant abode was in the mountains and tombs, as being solitary and unclean places, fit habitation for unclean spirits: And being likewise removed from the resort of men, they were more convenient for the devils to practise their hellish malice, unobserved, upon this poor creature. But I do not know, that common madmen are observed to frequent such places, more than others. If this man only laboured under

* Mark i. 12. The apostle's words are, *And immediately the spirit driveth him into the wilderness.* I am inclined to think, that this was the evil spirit; and our translators seem to think so too. They use the same expression in both places; and the original words in both places seem to have a near affinity to each other. The idea of *driving* sounds something harsh, and as such, seems more applicable to the evil spirit than to the gentle spirit of God; by whom Jesus was only *led into the wilderness.* Matt. iv. 1. Luke iv. 1. And why might not the evil spirit, when he found that was to be the place in which our Saviour was to be exposed to his temptations, and which he saw to be so favourable for the purpose, immediately strike-in with the design; and, out of eagerness to carry it into execution, add force to gentleness, and hurry him on to the scene of action? The term πνευμα is general, and common to both good and bad spirits.

some

some bodily diforders; according to this interpretation, if it be carried throughout, he muft have had a vaft complication of diftempers. If he had not a legion of devils, he muft have had other maladies and complaints, without number.

There are not furely fix thoufand fix hundred and fixty-fix kinds of madneffes; and I hope the human body, diftempered as it is, is not fubject to fo many diftempers of all kinds, as is here implied. The author of the Effay on Demoniacks takes notice of this objection to his hypothefis—" Can one " man have a legion of difeafes * ?" But offers nothing in anfwer to this queftion.

It is time to proceed to fome other cafes.

III. St. *Matthew* gives an account of *a dumb man, poffeffed with a devil*, who was brought to our Saviour; and *when the devil was caft out, the dumb fpake* †. This dumbnefs appears to have been caufed by the poffeffion, and removed by the difpoffeffion, when the man was reftored to the ufe of his fpeech. Here was no madnefs, nor epilepfy, nor any other natural diforder. The

* Effay, p. 312.
* Matt. ix. 32.

mul-

multitude marveled at the greatness of the miracle, saying, *It was never so seen in Israel.* Our Saviour had just before opened the eyes of two blind men; and if this dumbness was no more than a natural failure, or obstruction in the organs of speech, there could be nothing more wonderful in this miracle, than the two foregoing ones. But there was a possession in this case, which was not in the former ones. And the wonder lay in the dispossession, which being the first dispossession of the kind that our Saviour ever performed; the like to it might justly be said never to have been seen in *Israel.*

There were those among the *Jews* and heathens, who used charms and incantations for the cure of diseases. There were pretenders to exorcise, and cast out devils: And we have grounds to believe, there were such as sometimes succeeded in dispossessing them, by invoking the God of *Abraham, Isaac,* and *Jacob* over them. They all used certain forms, and rites, and ceremonies, in exorcising, which took up time; the success of which was at last doubtful; and at best was not immediately ascertained.

Our

Our Saviour inftantly caft out this devil, without any formal or tedious procefs, at a word's fpeaking; and with fuch circumftances, and in fuch a manner, as enforced conviction upon all who faw the miracle; the like to which they acknowledged had never been feen in *Ifrael*. The Jewifh exorcifts never undertook to eject devils, that deprived men of their fpeech. Here was a miraculous cure of that kind performed. The Pharifees could not deny the reality of it; but in their malice, they gave it a wrong turn, and afcribed it to a finifter caufe: They faid, *He cafteth out devils, through the prince of the devils* *.

It appears from the texts already quoted and referred to, that our Saviour had caft out a number of devils before this time. There was no difputing the truth of the facts: Nothing therefore was left for his enemies to do, but to deftroy the credit of them. For this purpofe, they racked their wits for fome objection againft thefe miracles: But in vain. The fcene of them was in *Galilee*, and the fame of them was fpread far and wide. It had reached *Jerufa-*

* Matt. ix. 34.

lem. The *Sanhedrim* probably was convened, and held a confultation on the occafion. This learned body confifted chiefly of the fcribes and doctors of their law; who having at length cooked up this objection, a deputation of them was fent with it to *Galilee*, to furnifh the *Pharifees* there with it. For it may be fairly traced up to the fcribes of *Jerufalem*; who, it is certain, were the immediate authors of it. Thus we are informed, that *the fcribes which came down from Jerufalem to Galilee*, faid, He hath Beelzebub, and by the prince of the devils, cafteth he out devils*.

They feem to have come on purpofe on this errand; for it doth not appear they had any other end for their journey. The objection is thrown out by them without reference to any preceding difpoffeffion; and the paffage in which it is contained, ftands alone, unconnected with what goes before, and likewife with any thing that follows, except our Saviour's reflections upon it.

It feems to have been defigned for a ftanding objection, to be ready for application on

* Mark iii. 22.

all future occasions. The first occasion that offered was that which is recorded in *Matthew* ix. 32. which we have been considering. It doth not appear that our Saviour was present at this time, when the Pharisees made this objection: But he had lately refuted it, when first made by the Scribes, to their faces; whence there was the less occasion for his taking notice of it again so soon after, if he was present; and therefore he might well answer it now, with the contempt which it deserved. This, however, gave the Pharisees confidence to urge it again, as we shall find hereafter; when our Lord found it necessary to put a stop to their triumphing in it, and to reason them out of it, by the power of his arguments.

It may give some satisfaction to know how these Jewish doctors themselves came by this curious objection.

And to me it pretty evidently appears, that it was not investigated by them out of the stores of their own rabbinical learning; but that they found it necessary to make a farther search, and were at last obliged to the heathen demonology for it. According to which,

which, whatever means were supposed to have any efficacy, either to sooth and conciliate, or else to drive away evil spirits, were all referred to *Pluto*, who was esteemed the prince of demons, on account of his supplying charms for this purpose*. And *Pluto* was the same with *Beelzebub*.

Here we plainly see the notion of overruling demons by the prince of the demons: And hence I doubt not the Scribes drew their objection of casting them out by the same power. But wherever they had it, or whoever were the authors of it; considered in itself, it appears to be a very ill one. The futility and absurdity of it is sufficiently exposed by our Saviour's reasoning, from an apt comparison to a house or kingdom divided against itself; whereby it must necessarily work its own downfall and destruction. This objection therefore militates against itself, and proves to be a *felo de se*.

On the other hand, this advantage accrues from this objection, that it is grounded upon

---

* Τους πονηρους δαιμονας ουκ εικη υπο τον Σαραπιν υποπτευομεν—ότι τα μειλισματα, και τα τελων αποτροπαια προς τον Πλουτωνα γινεται—Ὁ Θεος δια τετο μαλιστα δαιμονων αρχων, και συμβολα διδες προς την τετων ελασιν. Porph. apud Euseb. præp. evang. lib. iv. cap. 23.

a supposition of the reality of whatever dispossessions it is leveled against. For this would never have been admitted; had there been any the least flaw in it; or the least room to suspect the truth of the possession or dispossession; which the keen malice of these determined enemies would not fail to have found out. But as this was what they could not do; the strongest sanction is hereby given to the testimony of the other eye-witnesses of the miracle. And the Pharisees themselves condemn those, who at this distance of time dispute the reality of it.

I shall defer the farther consideration of this objection, till we come to the next case; under which our Saviour undertakes the thorough refutation of it; and shews the great guilt of the sin which is involved in it.

IV. St. *Matthew* informs us, that *there was brought unto Jesus one possessed with a devil, blind and dumb:* And that he *healed him, insomuch that the blind and dumb both spake and saw**.

* Matt. xii. 22..

St.

St. *Luke* represents this miracle in somewhat a different manner, which ascertains it no less. *And he was casting out a devil, and it was dumb: And it came to pass, when the devil was gone out, the dumb spake, and the people wondered*.*

According to this account, the devil was dumb himself, as well as the man; and in consequence of the devil's being cast out, the dumb man recovered his speech. The dumbness of the man was plainly caused by the devil. He was therefore justly punished with a deprivation of speech himself; and made to sympathize with him.

The man's dumbness was removed by our Saviour. Not so the devil's. He was no object of his mercy. We read of several devils, who spake in those whom they possessed; and were silenced by Christ. This was not permitted to speak at all: And both these dumb and silenced devils may

* Luke xi. 14. Some think the evangelists here give accounts of two different miracles, because, they say, the order of the history requires them so to be understood. See Macknight's Harmony, prelim. obs. p. 22. I am not for multiplying miracles: But if that be the case, it well accounts for the few differences of diction and matter which there are between the two relations.

be looked upon as typical of their oracles among the heathens, and prognosticating their being silenced and struck dumb, wherever the gospel was preached and planted; the time for which was approaching. They were indeed observed to be upon the decline, by the heathens themselves, for some time before *; having begun to shrink at the dawn of the gospel; which they could not account for.

The word in the original, which we translate *dumb*, literally signifies *deaf*†, in its primary sense; and is inclusive of being *dumb* too, in a consequential acceptation; which the context here determines it to; because the want of hearing is productive of the like defect in speech, when persons are born deaf. Not otherwise. This dumb man therefore was deaf likewise. And hence it may be inferred, that the devil deprived him of both these faculties from his very birth, or infancy: Which renders the miracle of restoring him to the use of them, together with that of his eye-sight, so much the greater.

* Cic. de Divinatione, lib. ii.
† Gr. κωφος.

This was so signal a miracle, that the people were convinced of it, to astonishment; and justly concluded, that the author of it could be no less a person than the son of David, the promised *Messiah*. The Pharisees could not help feeling the same conviction; but were quite destitute of the like candour and ingenuity. And, rather than they would suffer the miracle to have its proper effect upon their minds, they revived the former objection, of its having been performed by the assistance of *Beelzebub*; which, as it had not been taken notice of, in the last mentioned case, they hoped to entrench themselves safely in it; and flattered themselves with its being unanswerable.

I would here beg leave to observe, by the way, that notwithstanding the number and malice of our Saviour's enemies, we do not find the truth or reality of any one of these, or of his other miracles, in the least contested by them.

But, as in the present case, this miracle was ascribed to the prince of the devils; so in the following ages, the unbelieving Jews, being forced to admit the reality of his miracles in general, could find no other way to disparage them, than by objecting, that he wrought them by art magick, which he had learned in Egypt *.

To proceed. St. *Luke*, in his account of this miracle, relates, that while some said *he casteth out devils through Beelzebub the chief of the devils, others, tempting him, sought of him a sign from heaven* †; in confirmation of this sign upon earth. The *Scribes* and *Pharisees*, and *Sadducees* likewise, were very importunate for signs at every turn. But if it was any particular sign which they wanted, it no where appears what that sign was. There had been signs from heaven at Christ's nativity, and at his baptism; which probably they had heard of. Would nothing else satisfy them, unless some of these were repeated; or some such were exhibited at every turn before their eyes? Whatever the sign was, the demand of it was unreasonable, amidst the manifold signs and wonders which they daily saw. And therefore our Saviour did not think fit to gratify them. But as here was a palpable fact staring them in the face; the truth of which they durst not deny, they had no

* Vide Toldos Jeschu confut. apud Wagenseil, p 44.
† Luke xi. 15, 16.

the Case of the Gospel Demoniacks. 55

other shift left than to slight and deprecate it as much as they could; and by some means or other to divert the attention of the by-standers from it: And hence alone, I am persuaded, it was; that they evasively demanded another sign in confirmation of it; which implied an acknowledgement of its reality.

Our Saviour for the present takes no notice of the perverse demand: But proceeds to answer the main objection, of his casting out devils through *Beelzebub*; with regard to which, we are informed, that *he knew their thoughts.* He had heard and answered the objection before, as we have seen; by which means he, of course, acquired this knowledge, as he might have done, had he not been a discerner of thoughts, as he certainly was.

His first argument, in answer to the objection, hath been considered already. As the Pharisees persisted in it, he here adds a second, in which he argues with them on their own principles; and refutes them with their own opinion. *If I by Beelzebub cast out devils, by whom do your sons cast them out?*

out *? He still argues on the supposition of their being in reality cast out. There were, as observed above, some exorcists among themselves, whom they allowed to have the power of ejecting devils. If I eject them by *Beelzebub*, so may they; which yet you never objected to them. But, if they, as you believe, do it by the power of God, why may not I be allowed to do as much by the same power? *Therefore shall they be your judges.* I appeal to them—to your own sons; and am willing they should judge between us. And if they condemn you, and are in their own consciences convinced, that *I cast out devils by the finger of God; no doubt the kingdom of God is come upon you.* This is an indubitable proof of the arrival of his kingdom; which was now about to overtake that faithless generation; upon whom its judgements would soon be executed.

Our Saviour continues his discourse, and delivers a very useful point of doctrine, concerning the strength of *Satan*, and his own superior power, under the following very significant emblem.

* Luke xi. 19.

When a strong man armed keepeth his palace, his goods are in peace. But when a stronger than he shall come upon him, and overcome him, he taketh from him all his armour, wherein he trusted, and divideth his spoils *. The strong man armed we can suppose to be none other than the devil: Nor the stronger than he, to be any other than Christ.

The houses of the heathens, as well as their bodies, were full of devils, as they themselves confessed †. But the house, or palace here meant was the body of a man, such as that the devil had possessed, and was dispossessed of by Christ; a plain instance of his superior power over the great enemy of our salvation, whom our Saviour conquered, and turned out of his usurped possession; and gave his followers the benefit of the victory, to be distributed among them, here called dividing his spoils.

He concludes his discourse, by informing us, what the consequence of the devil's

---

* Luke xi. 21, 22.

† Και οικος δε πας μεςος—και τα σωματα τοινυν μεςα απο τατων. Porph. apud Euseb. præp. Evang. lib. iv. cap. 23.

being

being caft out of a man, who neglects co-operating with Chrift, to perfect the deliverance he wrought for him, fometimes is, for want of his refifting the devil, when releafed from him; and working out his own falvation with fear and trembling; as it is incumbent upon fuch a one to do above all others. He thereby fruftrates the mercy beftowed upon him. *He that is not with me,* fays Chrift on this occafion, *is againft me; and he that gathereth not with me, fcattereth.* The watchful enemy of mankind takes advantage of the remiffnefs of fuch a one, and finding none other fo fit for his purpofe, returns to the empty habitation; and not only re-enters it himfelf, *but takes with him feven other fpirits more wicked than himfelf,* to accompany, *and dwell there with him.* No wonder our Lord pronounces *the laft ftate of fuch a man* to be *worfe than the firft.* A feafonable warning to all reprobate Chriftians, who fall off from the grace given them.

It feems probable, that the man, out of whom the devil had been now caft, neglected to make the proper ufe of that mercy, on which the unclean fpirit made a re-entry into him; whereby he fuffered that difmal cataftrophe, which our Lord forefaw, saw, and thus forewarned him of. And this wretched man might have been a proper emblem of that incorrigible generation, on whom all Chrift's endeavours for their falvation were loft: In return for which, they only grew more hardened and impenitent; whereby their laft ftate likewife was worfe than the firft.

But what fignifies all this difcourfe and admonition about evil fpirits, if there were none fuch? and if the poffeffion was only imaginary?

If there was no devil caft out, to what purpofe was the debate between our Saviour and the *Pharifees* about it? For what end did he ufe fo many arguments, and take fuch pains to reafon with them? On this fuppofition, his reafoning was all ideal and fpeculative; and his doctrine, I dread to fpeak it, was falfe and groundlefs. Both his reafoning and doctrine were grounded on the reality of the fact: And if it was not real, both muft fall to the ground.

In a prudential view, would our Saviour give fuch a handle to his enemies for cavilling at him? The *Pharifees* were daily lying in wait *to catch him in his words* *; and

---

* Mark xii. 13. Luke xx. 20.

took counsel how they might entangle him in his talk*. Here was a fair opportunity for them, if he talked of things that had no real existence, not only to catch him in his talk, but to expose the falsehood of his pretences, by assuring the astonished multitude, that there was in truth no possession in the case;—that this was a vulgar error; and this man's ailment was no more than a common infirmity; though I do not know how they could have brought it under the heads of madness or epilepsy.

However, they might have charged Jesus with false facts, sham miracles, and false doctrine, if he pretended to cast out devils, when he did not; and taught the reality of possessions, when they were only imaginary. And how this charge could be refuted, on this supposition, I know not.

Beelzebub is placed at the head of possessing demons: And to shake the faith of possessions, it was found expedient to sink his character and consequence, as much as might be. *Beelzebub* is but the *Lord of flies*; and whatever power he may have over them, you are to

---

* Matt. xxii. 15.

infer,

infer, that such a poor devil can have but little influence upon men, to enter their bodies either himself, or by those that are under him.

Though *Beelzebub* is the prince of demons, yet it is asserted, and stiffly contended for, that he is not the devil. And yet he is not denied to be *Satan* *. For *Beelzebub* and *Satan* are convertible terms, and are used as such; and they are considered as the names of one and the same person, throughout the passage before us, in the three gospels. We cannot therefore avoid concluding them to be but two different names for the same Being. And *Satan* is the devil's proper name. Our Saviour called him by that name, when he was tempted by him. *Get thee hence, Satan* †. *Get thee behind me, Satan* ‡.

And when the other Evangelists say, Jesus was tempted of the devil, St. *Mark* says, he was *tempted* of *Satan* ||. In the *Apocalypse*, to ascertain him beyond all doubt or possibility of evasion, as one would

* Essay on Demoniacks, p. 16.
† Matt. iv. 10.
‡ Luke iv. 8.
|| Mark i. 13.

think,

think, he is called the devil, and *Satan*, more than once, together with such a description of him as suits no other Being in the universe.

The term *Satan* is applied to the devil about thirty three times in the New Testament; about six or seven in the Old; in all, about forty times, as his proper name: And therefore may surely be understood to be as much appropriated to him as any proper name can be to any person. Nor is it applied to any other, but once, as an appellative, to *Peter*; which our Saviour applies to him, by way of accommodation, as personating his adversary, by his ill suggestions. And he applies the term devil, in the same manner, to the traitor. In the *Revelation*, he is twice called by both these names together, the *devil* and *Satan*, the one being exegetically joined to the other; and he is described in each so particularly, as not to admit of any mistake, unless it be a wilful one. *The great dragon was cast out, that old serpent, called the Devil and Satan, which deceiveth the whole world. He was cast out into the earth: and his angels were cast out with him**. *And he laid hold on the dra-*

* Rev. xii. 9.

gon,

gon, that old serpent, which is the Devil and Satan, and bound him a thousand years *.

He and his angels being cast out may not improbably allude to their being cast out of the bodies of men, as well as to the downfall of their kingdom: and his being bound a thousand years is meant of a restriction of his power, in general, of every sort, both in this and other respects. The devil hath so many denominations given him, which are all characteristical of him, beyond all doubt or dispute; if there were not those who will dispute the plainest things in the world.

Satan is supposed to have a kingdom †: and accordingly is said to have a throne ‡. Surely all these instances and circumstances are characteristical enough of the devil; and sufficient to prove, that *Beelzebub* is none other than the devil himself, under that name.

Beelzebub is the prince of the demons: and the devil is the chief of the fallen angels.

† Rev. xx. 22.
* Matt. xii. 26.   Luke xi. 18.
‡ Rev. ii. 13. ὅπου ὁ θρόνος Σατανᾶ.

He is placed at the head of the principalities and powers, and of the rulers of darkness of this world ‡. And he seems to have no less power and authority than *Beelzebub*. Surely then the power is the same, the kingdom the same, and the person the same, that presides over it; unless we suppose there are two kingdoms of darkness; which I hope there are not. The subjects of this kingdom must therefore be the same. And, upon the whole, I think, the conclusion is unavoidable, that demons and fallen angels are the same kind of Beings; and that there is no foundation in scripture, for making any distinction between them: On the contrary, some proof will hereafter be given from scripture and antiquity, that the demons of the gospel are none other than apostate angels.

But there is behind matter of the most serious consideration of any that hath yet occurred.

Our Saviour pronounces a vey heavy judgement upon those, who ascribed his miracles of casting out devils to *Beelzebub*, the prince of the devils. He reckons their

* Ephes. vi. 12.

sin to be no less than blasphemy against the Holy Ghost, by whose power he wrought them; and this sin he pronounces to be irremissible. *All manner of sin and blasphemy shall be forgiven unto men; but the blasphemy against the Holy Ghost shall not be forgiven unto men* *.

To have a right apprehension of the nature and guilt of this great sin, and of the relation which it bears to the subject in hand; it should be considered, that the Holy Ghost visibly descended upon our Saviour Christ at his baptism;—that, upon his entrance into his ministry, before he wrought any of his miracles, he publickly, in the synagogue of his own city, *Nazareth*, applied that prophecy of *Isaiah* to himself—*The spirit of the Lord is upon me, because he hath appointed me*, among other purposes,. *to preach deliverance to the captives* of Satan; and to set at liberty them that are bruised †, and sore vexed by evil spirits possessing them. For this I take to be the most obvious and primary sense of the words. Consider farther, that

* Matt. xii. 31.
† Luke iv. 18. Isa. lxi. 1.

St. *Peter* appeals to all his hearers concerning *the word which they knew was published throughout all Judea, and began from Galilee; How God anointed Jesus of Nazareth with the Holy Ghost, and with power; who went about doing good, and healing all that were oppressed of the devil. For God was with him* *.

These were matters of fact of great notoriety—that our Saviour was baptized with the Holy Ghost—that, according to a prophecy, which he applied to himself, he was anointed with the Holy Ghost, and sent by God for many excellent purposes; and, among the rest, for this of delivering those that were held in captivity by Satan's possessing of them—that he publickly opened his commission for that end—and, in consequence of it, he assumed to cast out devils by the spirit of God; which was at once the fulfilling of this prophecy, and a most signal proof of it likewise.

Notwithstanding all this evidence, the *Pharisees* obstinately shut their eyes against it; and, on the contrary, maintained, that it was through *Beelzebub*, the prince of the

* Acts x. 37, 38.

devils, that Christ cast them out. Nay, they did not stick to say, that he had a devil himself*. And they repeated, and persisted in, this foul calumny: *Thou hast a devil. Say we not well, that thou art a Samaritan, and hast a devil* †? *He hath a devil, and is mad* ‡.

Hence, I apprehend, it appears, wherein the sin against the Holy Ghost properly consists. 1. In ascribing the works of God to the devil. And, 2. In the calumny of

---

* Jo. vii. 20. viii. 20.

† Jo. x. 20.

‡ These have been taken for synonymous terms, and the one as being exegetical of the other, supposing possession to denote no more than madness. But, as the Author of the Essay on Demoniacks rightly observes, " they are not necessarily to be understood as synonymous " terms; because possession may be put for the appre- " hended *cause*, and madness for the supposed effect." p. 93. And the malice of the Jews was such, that they would not stick to fasten the foulest calumny upon our blessed Saviour; and to reckon him not only mad, but that his madness was of the worst sort, even a diabolical one, proceeding from the devil, which they asserted was within him.

The fidelity of the historian is here remarkable, in recording what might be thought the greatest disparagement to his dear Lord and master, when the other evangelists had omitted it; and he might easily have suppressed it likewise.

F 2   alledging,

alledging, that the holy Jesus was possessed with a devil himself. St. *Mark* grounds it upon this bottom alone. *He that shall blaspheme against the Holy Ghost hath never forgiveness, but is in danger of eternal damnation: because they said, he hath an unclean spirit**. This was supposing, either that the spirit which he had was an unclean one, and that he had none other: Or else, that he had an unclean spirit, together with the holy Spirit of God. However it be understood, there could not be greater blasphemy.

It hath been observed, that even the charge of casting out devils by *Beelzebub* implied an acknowledgement, that they had been cast out by some means or other. The blasphemy contained in it implies it more strongly. Our Saviour's ascribing his casting out of devils to the Holy Ghost, not only supposes his casting of them out; but points out the power by which he did it. But now the denying of his casting of them out at all is a denial of the fact, which he assumed to perform; and is a virtual denial of the power, by which he did perform it; and it is likewise a denial of the doctrine

---

* Mark iii. 29, 30.

con-

concerning the unpardonable sin, which he here builds upon it.

Its being so unpardonable evinces the reality of the ejection, beyond all contradiction. For, if there were no evil spirits ejected, why should this be a sin of so deep a dye? Upon what grounds could it be called any sin at all?

So again, if this miracle is to be reduced to the level of other miracles, why is the disparaging of it in this manner to be thus distinguished, and loaded with so much guilt? If all that was done, was the restoring of a deaf and dumb man to his hearing and sight, why was the traducing of this miracle a more unpardonable sin, than it would have been, had any other miracles, which were not inferior to it, met with the like treatment? The superior guilt of the sin, as it shews the superiority of the miracle; so doth it more strongly ascertain the reality of the fact. For it must be a greater miracle, to cure a deaf and dumb man, and to cast out a devil too, than to cure a deaf and dumb man only.

Besides, to ascribe this miracle to *Beelzebub* could be no such great offence, if there were no *Beelzebub* to ascribe it to: But to ascribe it to him, and at the same time to deprive the Holy Ghoſt of the honour of it, made it ſo exceeding ſinful.

In a word, either acknowledge the facts, that our Saviour did caſt out devils; or elſe account for his doctrine concerning rhe irremiſſible nature of the ſin againſt the Holy Ghoſt, which ſeems to be built upon thoſe facts, in ſome other manner independently of them.

This, I am apt to think, was found to be an unſurmountable difficulty; and therefore was never attempted. The unpardonable ſin is totally overlooked, though interwoven with the miracle; and therefore ought, both on account of its connection, and of its importance, to have been particularly conſidered. But I do not recollect to have ſeen any mention made of the ſin, or of the Holy Ghoſt, throughout this performance.

The divinity of the Holy Ghoſt, and even his perſonality, is denied, I do not ſay by this writer, but by others of his principles: But we need not go any farther than the paſſage before us for the proof of both.

For if he can be offended, he muſt be a perſon; and he muſt be a divine perſon, to be offended ſo grievouſly: He muſt be very
God.

God. If he were not such, the sin of blaspheming him could not be so very great: It could not be greater, than that of blaspheming our Lord Christ; whom we believe to be very God likewise. We should beware of all approaches to this sin, as we tender our own salvation.

There is no one in these days, that can be so impious, as to attribute the works of God to the devil: But the spirit of grace may otherwise be done despite to.

The Son of God, who is all forgiveness, hath declared, that *whosoever speaketh a word against himself, it shall be forgiven him**: and to mitigate the offence, he here calls himself the Son of Man. Every true disciple of his will, notwithstanding, be very cautious of incurring it. It should therefore be seriously considered, whether the speaking of a word against his casting out devils by the Spirit of God, be not speaking against him, and that Divine Spirit too.

To his own master every man stand or falleth. But *there is a sin not unto death, which if we see a brother commit,* we are re-

* Matt. xii. 32.

quired to pray for him*. If any brother be guilty of this sin, he hath my most earnest prayers to God, that it may not be imputed to him, nor ever rise up in judgement against him.

V. Let us proceed to another instance. When our Saviour descended from the mount, after his transfiguration; a man brought him his only child, whom St. *Matthew* calls a lunatick: But his lunacy appears to have been the effect of a diabolical possession. For when our Saviour cast out the devil, the child was cured from that very hour †. Lunacy is a distemper, so called, from its periodical returns, in which it is supposed to be influenced by the moon. This child is therefore said to have been cured *from that very hour*, to indicate a cure so perfect, that he never afterwards had any returns of his disorder at all; pursuant to Christ's charge, *Come out of him, and enter no more into him* ‡. According to St. *Mark's* account, the youth's father called this *a dumb spirit*, which he had *of a child*. Our Saviour calls it *a dumb and deaf spirit*. Whence it ap-

---

* 1 Jo. v. 16.
† Matt. xvii. 14.
‡ Mark ix. 14.

pears, that his dumbness proceeded from his deafness; as he was deaf from his infancy. This confirms an observation made above in a like case *.

Both *Mark* and *Luke* call this a foul and unclean spirit. They all describe the sufferings of the poor young man, as being very severe, and expressly ascribe them to this wicked spirit. *He taketh him, and teareth him, and bruising him, hardly departeth from him. And it oft times hath cast him into the fire, and into the waters, to destroy him; and tare,* or rather convulsed, *him, and rent him sore in our Lord's presence* †. When the spirit came out of him, the young man was *as one dead, insomuch, that many said he was dead.* It had taken such strong hold of him, that the disciples could not cast him out; though it doth not appear they ever had failed before. It was a spirit, it seems, of a particular kind, and so obstinate, as not to be expelled, but by prayer and fasting; some intenseness and severity of devotion and mortification being requisite for the purpose.

* See p. 52.
† Mark ix. 22. Luke ix. 39. 42.

Our Saviour had juft then been at his devotions on the mount; which undoubtedly were accompanied with fafting; when forefeeing this great object of his mercy would be prefented to him, he particularly prayed the Father for power to relieve him. It appears farther, that an extraordinary faith was alfo requifite for cafting out this kind of fpirit; as our Lord upbraided his difciples for their want of it on this occafion. This likewife, as is generally the cafe, was attended with a neglect of their devotional duties, during his abfence from them. The ill fuccefs of the difciples had made the young man's father almoft defpair of Chrift's power to relieve him. *If thou canft do any thing, have compaffion on us, and help us.*

The bufy inquifitivenefs of the *Scribes*, on this occafion, wherein they feem to have taken advantage of our Saviour's abfence, gave them an opportunity of informing themfelves of the nature of the cafe, and the reality of the poffeffion; as well as to enquire into the pretenfions of the difciples, and perhaps their Lord's likewife, to a power over evil fpirits; which afforded them withal the malicious pleafure of infulting the

dif-

disciples upon their miscarriage. But when our Lord asked them, what they were questioning about, they were awed into silence. There was likewise a great concourse of people on this occasion; who all became witnesses of the fact; and were all amazed at the mighty power of God.

Now here are so many remarkable circumstances in this case, all concurring to establish the truth and reality of the possession, that seem to be sufficient to convince the most hardened unbeliever.

The *Scribes*, we see, were silenced, if not convinced, by it. They were the learned of the nation. They were sufficiently prejudiced against our Lord, on all occasions. They were always upon the watch, and soon heard of the disciples' miscarriage; which brought them instantly to the place, in hopes now of triumphing over them for their disgrace. But even while they lay under it, before the devil was cast out, our Saviour gave them a fair challenge to declare their scruples, if they had any. But as they had nothing to say, either then, or after the miracle had been wrought; what stronger presumption can there be of the truth of it? And with how ill a grace is it now contested?

contested? Have these moderns better means or opportunities of examining into it than those *Scribes* had, who were so well qualified and inclined; and had come there for that very purpose?

If the belief of these possessions was a vulgar error, this was the time, and these the persons, for exposing and refuting it. If the learned and unlearned were all equally persuaded of it, and were confirmed in the persuasion, by so many extraordinary facts, on what grounds do we now raise any questions about it?

When the disciples asked our Saviour privately, why they could not cast the devil out? If there had been no devil in the case, why did he not communicate the secret to them in confidence? If it was to be made a secret of to the multitude; which I do not see the least reason for; but all the reason in the world to the contrary. Were the disciples, to whom he revealed and explained other mysteries, not then proper to be divulged to the croud of his audience? Were they not to be entrusted with this *esoterick* doctrine? Were they, who were gradually to be led into all truth, to be confirmed in this error?—A religious error, which it so nearly

nearly concerned them, of all others, to be undeceived in; who were to be the special preachers of the gospel of truth to the world. It appears, that after the spirit of truth came, who guided them into all truth, they held the same doctrine; used the same language concerning it; and followed the same practice of casting out devils, pursuant to their commission; and after the example, which had been set them by their Master, as we have seen in part already, and shall see farther presently.

What occasion was there for our Saviour to say any thing about this or that kind of devils; if there were no devils of any kind to be cast out? If he thought proper to conform to the vulgar language, why should he be so particular in confirming the vulgar error? If this was no more than a common epilepsy, what was there in that distemper, for the cure of which so much fasting and prayer, and so much faith too, was requisite, more than for the removing of other distempers? But faith in what? Not surely, that there was no devil to be cast out: But that there really and truly was: Otherwise, why should they be so severely reproved by our Saviour for the want of it? O *faithless and*

and perverfe generation! How long fhall I be with you? How long fhall I fuffer you*? But wherein lay their fault, if there was no devil to be ejected? Were they upbraided for not believing a thing to be, which never had any exiftence?

The young man's father afcribed his fon's diftemper to a fpirit, which he calls a dumb one. It is obferved already, that the difciples having failed to caft him out, had made the man rather diffident of their mafter's power to do it; which was the reafon why he did not bring his fon with him to our Saviour, when he addreffed him about him. Hence Chrift infifted on the man's faith, as well as that of the difciples; and very properly, if there was a devil to be caft out: But furely not otherwife. For if there was no devil in the cafe, he never

---

* Some underftand thofe words as directed to the Scribes: But though they are very applicable to them; yet as neither St. *Matthew* nor *Luke* take any notice of them, in their accounts; and thefe words notwithftanding occur in thefe evangelifts, as well as in St. *Mark*, who alone makes any mention of the Scribes; and as the words are fpoken with regard to the inability of the difciples, for want of faith, to caft out this foul fpirit; I do not fee how they can be otherwife underftood than as meant of them. See Macknight's Harmony in loc. fect. 73.

could

could have excited this act of faith in the man; nor given him any assurance concerning it. *If thou canst believe, all things are possible to him that believeth.* The father having, with tears, instantly expressed his faith; and besought Christ to help the weakness of it, Jesus rebuked the evil spirit; saying unto him, in the presence of a great concourse of people, *Thou dumb and deaf spirit; I charge thee to come out of him; and enter no more into him.* Was this language to be used for the cure of a natural distemper?

I would only beg leave to observe farther, that the inveteracy, as well as the obstinacy, of the case concurred in establishing the reality of the possession. For he had it from a child. The difficulty of the cure confirmed it. The uncommonness of it made it the more to be taken notice of. And the absoluteness of the cure manifested the greatness of the miracle in the dispossession. And the genuine marks of truth appear throughout the whole.

VI. The case of the *Syro-phœnician* woman's daughter[*] is not to be passed unnoticed.

The notion of diabolical possessions was not peculiar to the *Jews;* nor particularly

---

[*] Matt. xv. 21. Mark vii. 25.

grounded

grounded upon the *Jewish* scriptures. It had overspread the gentile world likewise; and was founded upon the woeful experience of the one, as well as the other. This woman was an instance of it. She was a *Greek*, or *Gentile*; a *Syro-phenician*, or *Canaanite*, by nation; whereby she is sufficiently distinguished from the *Jews*; and this is confirmed by the whole conversation which passed between Christ and her. She had notwithstanding heard so much of his fame, for the cure of diabolical possessions, that having a young daughter, who had an unclean spirit, she came, and fell at the feet of *Jesus*; and besought him to cast forth the devil out of her; with which she was grievously vexed. Our Saviour at first seemed to turn a deaf ear to her; and remonstrated against her request; as she was not a proper object of his mercy; having been *sent only to the lost sheep of the house of Israel*. But at length the importunity of the disciples; together with her own earnest supplication; the strength of her faith; and the cogency of her reasoning, prevailed with him to grant her request; though out of the ordinary rules of his mission: And he dismissed her, with this comfortable assurance; that the devil was
gone

gone out of her daughter; who had been made whole from that very hour; as the mother found to her great joy, when she returned to her house.

Now is it possible to conceive; that all this was no more than a piece of scenery; and that there was not here any real possession; when the whole conversation, which is very entertaining, as well as affecting, turns upon the truth and reality of it? The woman came to our Saviour under a strong persuasion of the possession: Did he do, or say, any thing to undeceive her? Did not his whole conduct indicate the contrary? He knew what he meant to do from the beginning. His remonstrances were not designed to destroy, or lessen, her faith in this great point; but to heighten and increase it. And when he had worked it up to its proper pitch, he dismissed her with this testimony, *O woman, great is thy faith: Be it unto thee even as thou wilt.*

Faith was the general principle, on which our blessed Lord founded his religion. This consisted of several particulars, of which that under consideration is one; namely faith in his power of working miracles in general, and this of his casting out devils

devils particularly. Would he, who was truth itself, give any countenance to a falsehood? Would he confirm, and even heighten it, and that both by word and deed? The thought is impious to the last degree.

Blessed Lord! How art thou crucified afresh! How is thy word abused! There is not a book in the world, with which such liberties are taken.

I desire it may be observed, that here is no one distemper mentioned, as connected with this case; or that it can be resolved into, more than another.

There are two or three particular cases more, which it may be proper to take notice of.

VII. What think you of the case of *Mary Magdalene*, out of whom our Saviour is said to have cast seven devils *? We have seen accounts of other complicated cases of this kind; one particularly of a man who had a legion of devils cast out of him. And our Saviour describes the case of a man, out of whom an unclean spirit went, and returned with seven others, to take possession of him again.

* Mark xvi. 9. Luke viii. 2.

The last state of such a man, when the unclean spirit re-entered him, together with so many others more wicked than himself, might well be said to have been worse than the first; when no more than one had taken possession of him.

Agreeably hereto we may conclude, That *Mary Magdalene* had been a great and enormous sinner: But that, in consequence of her having had such a number of devils cast out of her, she became a sincere penitent; and a true convert to Christ; which is confirmed to us by every thing we learn concerning her: And she hath accordingly been always looked upon in the church, as a most eminent example of a repenting sinner.

But we find not a word of any distemper, much less of any complication of distempers, which she laboured under; and had been cured of: Any more than we do of either of the above-mentioned persons; who, though they were possessed with so many evil spirits, are not supposed to have had any bodily distemper, but what was caused by them.

Are we notwithstanding to conclude, that all we read of these persons is to be understood

stood of no more than some ill state of health, or natural disorder? And that the man particularly, who had seven devils, only once recovered his health, and relapsed again, and was seized with many other and worse distempers than he had before? What moral instruction is here conveyed? Or, to what purpose is such a case mentioned at all? Are we not under a necessity of understanding this of his spiritual state; which if thus described to have been so extremely dangerous; when he was in this manner fallen into the power and possession of his spiritual enemies? This is supposed by some to be emblematical of the state of the reprobate *Jews*, of whom *Satan* took more durable possession; and rendered them seven times more the children of hell than they were before*.

But that even such a case is not quite desperate, beyond a possibility of recovery, the merciful *Jesus* hath given us an actual proof, that he hath in fact rescued a poor sinner out of the jaws of those direful fiends, and taken her under his own banner and protection; from thenceforth to keep her house, not empty, or destitute of divine grace and support; but swept from all filthy lusts; and

---

* See Whitby on Luke xi. 26.

garnished

garnished with the graces of the holy spirit: Whereby she should be enabled to withstand, and triumph over all the efforts of her spiritual enemies.

The turn that is given to this account of *Mary Magdalene's* having seven devils is, that she was *a distracted woman**. And from whom is this representation of her case taken; but from one of the bitterest enemies which christianity ever had? *Celsus* calls her γυνη παροιςρος † : And this is thought sufficient to discredit the plain gospel account of her case; which it hath no more relation to, than any other disorder that might occur to the infamous slanderer's imagination. But I am truly grieved to find this calumny catched up, and fastned upon her by a minister of *Christ*. Ori-

---

* Essay on Demoniacks, p. 105.

† The whole sentence is Γυνη παροιςρος, ὡς φασι. the literal translation of which is, *Mulier fanatica, ut dicitis*, a distracted woman, as you say, or as the saying is; of the same import with ὡς φημι, ὡς λογος, ὡς επος, ὡν επος ειπειν. I will not deny but that *Celsus* might intend to insinuate, by this mode of expression, as his translator understands him, that the christians acknowledged, the woman was disturbed in her senses; but he durst not charge them plainly with it, as it appears he had no foundation for it. Origen contra Celsum, lib. ii. p. 96.

gen, he might have seen, if he had read a little farther, is at a loss to find whence *Celsus* got any handle for the slander; there being, as he says, no foundation for it in the gospel history: Nor did he know of any such tradition about her; otherwise he would not have failed to take notice of it.

But if, in the case before us, it could be supposed that St. *Luke*, in the course of his history, might think fit to say, in conformity to the vulgar notion, that seven devils went out of her, when she had not so much as one in her; what need had St. *Mark* to go so far out of his way, on an occasion which did not seem to require it, as to say that *Jesus* had cast seven devils out of her? For he introduces it in a kind of parenthesis; and the sense had been complete without it. But he wrote, as he thought; and as the evangelists, and all other honest historians, must be supposed to do.

And the reason why he recorded the fact in this place, at the close of his gospel, seems to have been, because he had omitted to do it in the course of the history: Otherwise the bare mention of her name here had been sufficient to ascertain her person,

without

without the addition of that circumstance.

But when it is moreover said, that Christ distinguished that woman, out of whom he had cast seven devils, by appearing first to her * after his resurrection—when he talked, and revealed himself to her, and honoured her with the special trust of conveying the first news of his resurrection to his other disciples; and the first notice likewise of his intended ascension †;—All this indicates much confidence, as well as great approbation of her whole character and behaviour, since her conversion; suitably to that of a sincere penitent, as she hath always been esteemed.

But if we only look upon her in the light of a mad woman, cured by the charity of *Christ*; what merit could this be in her? Nor could her subsequent behaviour; were it ever so good and grateful for such a mercy, be paralleled with that of a repenting sinner; for whom there is so much joy in heaven.

But above all things; had this woman ever been disturbed in her senses, *Christ*

---
* Mark xvi. 9.
† Jo. xx. 11—18.

would never have pitched upon her, of all others, to carry the tidings of his resurrection to the apostles; lest they should suspect she had returned to one of her raving fits; since as it was, when she, with several other women, who never were under any such imputation, *told them these things; their words seemed to them as idle tales; and they believed them not* *.

Enough hath been said to vindicate this woman's character from the aspersion of *Celsus*. I am sorry any christian should give occasion for it.

VIII. There is a case of another woman, which is not foreign to this inquiry: I mean that of the woman, who was *bowed together with a spirit of infirmity eighteen years,* in such a manner, that *she could in no wise lift up herself* †. Upon whom our Saviour laid his hands, *and immediately she was made straight, and glorified God.*

It might be pleaded, that this was no more than an infirmity, which proceeded from some natural cause; had not our Saviour himself expressly ascribed it to *Satan*. *Ought not this woman, being a daughter of*

---

* Luke xxiv. 10, 11.
† Ibid. xiii. 11.

Abraham,

Abraham, whom Satan hath bound, lo, these eighteen years, be loosed from this bond on the Sabbath day? This spirit of infirmity, therefore, was an evil spirit, which caused it: And that no inferior demon, but *Satan* himself, who thus bowed her together; and kept her under this unmerciful bondage so long, till *Christ*, in his mercy, instantly released her from it. The poor woman was so sensible of the benefit; that she glorified God for it.

But the ruler of the synagogue took such offence, that Christ should do this on the Sabbath, that his indignation was raised at it—an indignation instigated by envy; for which our Saviour reprimanded the hypocrite so severely, that he, and all our Lord's adversaries were ashamed: When all the people, who were under no prejudice against him, rejoiced for all the glorious things that were done by him.

This case, in strictness of speech, cannot perhaps be called a possession, so properly as an obsession: But this was so constant and cruel an obsession, as to be little inferior to a possession; and was a standing proof of its own reality.

It hath been well obferved; "That fometimes by concurring with, and fometimes "without, natural caufes, many difeafes "were, by divine permiffion, brought on, "even by evil fpirits; which the gofpel, "and the hiftories of *Job* and *Saul* inform "us of*." Whofe cafes will be confidered at large hereafter. This the heathens likewife were fenfible of, and acknowledged; of which fome proof will be given in its proper place.

This woman, in her infirm condition, may ferve as a lively emblem of man in this his ftate of weaknefs and depravity; when he is under fuch fore bondage to *Satan*, that he cannot either lift up his hand to relieve himfelf; nor fo much as his heart to pray for relief from God: Till fuch time, as he takes compaffion on him; and bids him be loofed from his infirmity; as our Saviour was pleafed to fay unto the woman: And as, upon his fpeaking the word, and laying his hand upon her, fhe immediately was made ftraight, and glorified God: So then, and not till then, can our crooked and perverfe wills be rectified,

---

* Whitby on Luke xiii. 16.

so as that we may be able to lift up our minds to heaven, to praise and adore our Maker.

IX. I find but one other particular case of demoniacal possession in the gospel. And this is a case of such importance, that it should not by any means be omitted. It is that of the traitor *Judas*. Of him, St. *Luke* saith, that *Satan entered into him**. St. *John* likewise, though he takes no notice of any other demoniacal possessions, as he seldom mentions what had been recorded by the other evangelists; yet with regard to this, he says, that *Judas was*, διαβολος, *a devil*†. That the devil, διαβολος, again, had put it into his heart to betray his master ‡. And that when *Jesus* had given him the sop, *Satan* immediately entered into him ‖: Thus specifying the very instant of time, when the devil himself took possession of him.

Now here is a direct proof of the devil, in person, the chief of the fallen angels,

* Luke xxii 3.
† Jo. vi. 70.
‡ Chap. xiii. 2.
‖ Chap. xiii. 27.

by his acknowledged name, διαβολος, and not δαιμων, entering into, and taking possession of the body of a man. For by comparing these several texts together, men must be strongly disposed to cavil, if they will not acknowledge, that the devil and *Satan* are here one and the same: And it will surely be allowed, that the devil himself entered into *Judas*, if he ever entered into any man; had we not been so expressly informed of it.

This was business of such consequence, that the devil would not entrust any inferior wicked spirit, or *demon*, with it; and therefore he chose to perform it himself in person. Now here is an instance that comes fully up to the case in point. I would therefore fain know, what shifts can possibly be found to evade the force of this testimony. As here is no room to suppose, that any other evil spirit was concerned, but the arch-rebel himself; so there seems to be as little pretence for imagining, that there was any thing of a distemper in the case.

For, from all that is said about him, the man appears to have been in full health,

both

both before, and after the tranfaction here related. And it farther very plainly appears, that the devil continued in poffeffion of him, from the laft defperate act which he committed, in putting an end to his own wretched life, which undoubtedly was by the devil's inftigation; as he was a murderer from the beginning: Nor can any man deny, that many, of the felf-murders, which, to the reproach of humanity, as well as religion, are fo frequently perpetrated among us in thefe days, are not inftigated by him: Which are all unnatural, and fome fo unaccountable, that they cannot be imputed to any other caufe.

The nature of this cafe did not admit of any difpoffeffion; and hence the difmal confequences of it.

I would here obferve, that, as in this place, the devil and *Satan* appear to be the fame, this is an additional proof to fuch as are offered above*, that the devil, *Satan*, and *Beelzebub*, are but different names for this fame prince of the apoftate angels; which ferve the better to afcertain him, notwithftanding

---

* P. 62.

withstanding all the endeavours that have been used to the contrary.

The devil had from the beginning counteracted the proceedings of our Saviour, for the destruction of his kingdom; and to this end had assaulted him with his temptations, in order to draw him into sin; whereby he would have been disabled from becoming a Redeemer to mankind, as he should then stand in need of redemption himself. But, when he saw our Lord was not only able to withstand, and defeat all his assaults; but was going on conquering, and to conquer; every where dispossessing evil spirits, and freeing men from the miserable captivity, in which, by these his emissaries, *Satan* held them; whereby his power over them was daily diminishing, and his kingdom falling into decay, and in danger of being overthrown.—Being reduced to this desperate state, he had still one resource left, which, if he could succeed in, he concluded would be decisive; and this was no less, than to compass the destruction of this his powerful adversary; which therefore he was determined to attempt.

To this end, he found he could not make use of any more probable means, than by contriving to have him delivered into the hands of his enemies, whom he saw thirsting for his blood. And finding an instrument fit for his purpose, *the devil put it into the heart of Judas Iscariot to betray him* to them*. This was an important crisis. *This was the hour, and the power of darkness.* †. *He that had the power of death was the devil* ‡. This power he did not fail to enforce on this occasion. To render it effectual, he had the boldness to enter into the body of one of our Lord's chief disciples in person; lest the design should miscarry in the hands of any Being of inferior malice and abilities.

It doth not indeed appear, that any infernal spirit, but the devil himself, had the power of death delegated to him. And he had it no otherwise, in this case, than by permission to instigate wicked men to carry it into execution. It was therefore very suitable to his whole design, that he should literally enter into the body of the traitor, for this purpose; who having delivered his

---

* Jo. xiii. 2.
† Luke xxii. 53.
‡ Heb. ii. 14.

Master into the hands of his enemies, his grand adversary concluded, he should triumph over the captain of our salvation in the end.

But that turned out to his own destruction. For Christ, even *through his own death, destroyed him that had the power of death; that is, the devil; and delivered them who had been all their life-time subject to his bondage**, in this, and other respects.

I have been the longer in endeavouring to evince the reality of this possession, and the grounds of it, from its suitableness to the design and interest of the great enemy of mankind. And, if we allow a real possession in this case, the like will follow in others. The purpose of this possession was to instigate a base wretch to a very ungrateful and villainous act of treachery, and in analogy to it, the end and intent of all other diabolical possessions must have been to corrupt and pervert the hearts and minds of men, in some manner, and to some wicked purpose, or other.

But how comparatively low a sense of this part of scripture-history must it be, to

---

* Heb. ii. 14, 15. See Essay on Redemption, chap. xi. p. 216. 2d edit.

understand all these possessions, as merely fanciful; and as denoting no more, than some bodily distemper; and that even in the case of the traitor *Judas?*

We have had now a pretty full view of the gospel account of demoniacks, general and particular; every relation of which carries such special marks of reality, as leave not the least room to doubt about it. The circumstances of every separate possession, severally considered, ascertain the fact; and the contrary supposition, that these possessions were only fictitious, or imaginary, when severally applied to each, appear to be replete with absurdities.

There are three, or four accounts more of demoniacks, which we find in the *Acts of the apostles*; and which it will be proper here to subjoin, and take some notice of; in order to complete this enquiry.

X. The first that occurs is of a general nature; concerning which we read, that *there came a multitude out of the cities round about Jerusalem, bringing sick folks, and them which were vexed with unclean spirits; and they were healed every one,* by *Peter,* and the rest of the apostles; to whom they had been brought for that purpose.

These beneficent deeds provoked the indignation of the high-prieſt, *and of all them that were with him; which is the ſect of the Sadducees,* to that degree, that they committed the authors of them to the common priſon*.

It is very remarkable, that in all the goſpel accounts of the ejection of evil ſpirits, which were often cavilled at by the *Scribes* and *Phariſees,* we never once find any mention made of the *Sadducees,* as raiſing any objections againſt them, or concerning themſelves at all about them. On the contrary, we find a total ſilence in them relating to this matter.

I do not really know, how this can be accounted for otherwiſe, than from the inconteſtable marks of reality, which theſe miracles carried. For it appears from the place before us, that they did not want inclination to cavil at them, if they had found room; when their malice prompted them, one and all, to concur in impriſoning the apoſtles for theſe charitable offices; without being able to aſſign any cauſe, or pretence, for ſuch violent and injurious

* Acts v. 16, 17, 18.

treatment; especially, when it is confidered, that they were from principle likewife difpofed to difpute this power of cafting out devils, whoever undertook to do it. For it is well known, that the *Sadducees* denied the exiftence of either angels or fpirits*; good or bad; and confequently there could be, in their eftimation or belief, no fuch Beings as evil fpirits, to enter, or to be caft out of, the bodies of men.

When therefore they faw, or were informed, that the apoftles affumed to heal them that were vexed with unclean fpirits; this was their time for avowing their principles, and declaring, that the doctrine of diabolical poffeffions was no more than a vulgar error—that in reality there was no fuch thing—but that it was all fancy and imagination—and that thofe who pretended to it were downright impoftors; which they might have alledged, as a plaufible pretence for imprifoning of them.

But we do not find a fyllable of this. They were quite referved in declaring their opinion; becaufe it was, on this occafion, refuted by palpable facts, which ftared them

---

* Acts xxiii. 8.

in the face; which they durst not deny; nor could otherwise withstand, than by imprisoning the authors, in order to suppress the practice, and deter them from proceeding in works, which reflected so much disgrace upom them, and their principles: Though in vain; for the apostles, being miraculously released out of prison, had this divine attestation of the truth of the astonishing cures which they performed; and boldly justified themselves, and their works, when convened before the council *.

XI. *Philip*, the dracon, having gone down to *Samaria*, and preached Christ there; among other miracles which he wrought, caused *unclean spirits, crying with a loud voice, to come out of many, that were possessed with them*, to the great joy of that city †.

But what is most remarkable here, is the case of *Simon*, surnamed *Simon Magus*. This man had for *a long time before bewitched the people of Samaria, with his sorceries, giving out, that himself was some great one: To whom they all, from the least to the greatest, gave such heed, and paid such regard*, that they called him, *The great power of God*.

* Acts v. 13.
† Acts viii. 5—13.

Yet

Yet this man, who was so practised in the arts of magick and sorcery; and of course so conversant with evil spirits; seeing them forced out of the bodies of men, in so publick a manner, and *crying out with a loud voice*, at their expulsion, was so convinced of the power of *Philip* over them, that he, *though his heart was not right in the sight of God*, yet *believed, and was baptized* among many others, and *continued with Philip, wondering, and beholding*, these, and the other *miracles and signs, which were done* by him.

Now here is a case differing from all that we have seen, or shall see hereafter. A man, in confederacy with evil spirits, becomes a witness to their expulsion out of the bodies of men; though he still continued *in the gall of bitterness* against that power, by which they were expelled; as appears by the sequel of his story. What is conviction, if this be not?

XII. The next of these cases which we meet with, is that of *a damsel, possessed with a spirit of divination; which brought her masters much gain by sooth-saying**. This spirit of divination was a kind of familiar

* Acts xvi. 16.

spirit, or *demon*; by which such as it possessed, related many strange things; and undertook to foretel future events.

These were much resorted to by superstitious people; and a profitable trade was made of such pretensions.

This *Pythoness*, it seems, belonged to a company; who found their account in her, from the profit which she brought them. But this damsel, instead of divining, was moved to bear testimony to the apostles of Christ, *saying, these men are the servants of the Most High God; which shew unto us the way of salvation**. And this she persevered to do many days. Though she attested nothing but the truth, and what seemed to be for their honour, and the advantage of the cause they were embarked in; yet St. *Paul* was by no means pleased with such company; nor did he want the support of such a witness. *He was grieved* at the flattering attestation of a wicked spirit, which was given with no other intent, than to court the indulgence and forbearance of *Paul* from dispossessing him; agreeably to the like arts, which we have seen were used by evil spirits towards our Saviour.

* Acts xvi. 17.

St. *Paul* might be grieved likewise at the trouble which he foresaw, he, and his fellow labourer *Silas*, would fall into; and the disturbance which would be raised in the city, should he cast out this wicked spirit; which his duty obliged him to do. For as Christ had commissioned his apostles to cast out devils; and St. *Paul*, who *was not a whit behind the very chiefest of them*, in any respect, was to execute his commission on all occasions; and to cast out devils, wherever he met with them: Therefore, resolving at length to exert his authority, *he turned, and said to the spirit, I command thee, in the name of Jesus Christ, to come out of her: And he came out the same hour.* The consequence was such, as St. *Paul* apprehended. The masters of this damsel, enraged at their loss, when *they saw that all their gain was gone*, seized and dragged *Paul* and *Silas* into the market-place—brought them before the magistrates — raised the mob against them—caused them to be stripped, beaten, and closely confined in prison; and chained down like the greatest malefactors.

Now was there here no real possession?— No spirit of divination? If not, what was it that *Paul* cast out? And what was all this ftir about? The owners of the damfel were convinced of the difpoffeffion by an argument, generally the moft convincing and powerful of all others—that which affected their felf-intereft. When they faw, that their trade was fpoiled, and their profit all at an end, they were exafperated to the laft degree againft thofe that deprived them of it; who feverely felt the proofs of their conviction, as we have juft now feen.

But how can we account for St. *Paul's* conduct, if this damfel had no fpirit of divination? This was no rafh act. He had many days to deliberate about it. Why therefore fhould he embarrafs himfelf and his friend, in this manner, about a thing of nothing? Had he, of all men living, any need to court perfecution? If this woman only practifed footh-faying from a fanciful opinion, which fhe and others had taken up, that fhe had fome fkill in this art; where was the harm in fuffering her to join him and his company for fome days; and in bearing teftimony to them, which was fo full and honourable, however fhe came by it? If the *Pythoness* was only mad and raving; *Paul* could not be in his fober fenfes, to concern himfelf at all about her; much

lefs

less to run himself, and his fellow-labourer, into so much danger and suffering—for what? Not to cure a mad woman; but indeed to silence a woman that uttered the words of truth and soberness. For whatever her character and behaviour were in other respects; and however she expressed herself at other times; such were the only words which she spake on this occasion. And that is a strange proof of insanity, which is fetcht from her steady repetition of that which was none other than a great and most indubitable truth: Which yet is the only evidence of her insanity that is hinted at, or insinuated*.

In a word, the damsel's masters thought she had a spirit of divination: All the magistrates and people of *Philippi*, who were heathens, thought so. *Paul* and *Silas* thought so, who were originally *Jews*: And St. *Luke*, who wrote this history, thought so likewise; if there be any truth in history—if any regard is to be paid to it; or difference to be made between it and fable.

XIII. There is one other case in the *Acts of the Apostles*, which deserves to be taken

* Essay on Demoniacks, p. 107.

notice

notice of. It is that of the Jewish exorcists. *Then certain of the vagabond Jews, exorcists, took upon them to call over them, which had evil spirits, the name of the Lord Jesus; saying, we adjure you by Jesus, whom Paul preacheth* *.

These Jewish exorcists, it seems, made a trade of going about to exorcise such as were possessed by evil spirits; and we are here told, there were no fewer than seven sons of one man, *Sceva*, a *Jew*; and a chief of the priestly family, who practised this art: Whence it appears, that these possessions must have been very frequent in those days; and this trade of exorcising very profitable.

The *Jews* were used to exorcise, in the name of the God of *Abraham*, *Isaac*, and *Jacob*: But whatever success their exorcisms had been attended with, in the time before the gospel age; they seem not to have been very successful, since the commencement of it; as those men found it expedient to change the terms, and the names, through which they made their adjurations, for the name of *Jesus*: For observing how effectually *Paul* cast out devils in the name of *Jesus*; they also were tempted to make trial of the power of his name for this purpose; by invoking

* Acts xix. 13.

it over evil spirits, and adjuring them by *Jesus, whom Paul preached.* And they kept themselves united together, in hopes of prevailing by their numbers.

But *the evil spirit answered and said, Jesus I know, and Paul I know*—I have experienced their power to my cost. But *who are ye?* I disclaim your authority. You are no disciples of *Jesus;* nor have you any commission from him. Therefore, *the man, in whom the evil spirit was, leaped on them; and overcame them; and prevailed against them; so that they fled out of that house, naked and wounded* *.

It will be readily said, that this was no more than a common madman. But he must have had uncommon strength, thus to overcome so many men in a body; and to clear the house of them, with such marks of his rage upon them. These were experienced persons in demoniacal cases; whereby they were the better qualified for judging of the efficacy of those *special miracles,* which *God wrought by the hands of Paul,* in this respect; and of the reality of the cures which had been performed upon demoniacks, in consequence of the handkerchiefs and aprons

* Acts xix. 15, 16.

which had been brought from his body for that purpose *.

They undoubtedly took this man for a real demoniack; otherwise they never would have attempted his cure. This alone was what they professed; nor was madness, as such, any object of their undertaking. It appears by the consequence, that they were not mistaken in the case; as they carried such proofs of the possession about them. And it would be difficult to convince any one, who should put himself in their place, that this man was actuated only by a common phrenzy.

Jesus, says he, *I know, and Paul I know*. What knowledge could a madman have of either? And how unsuitable would such language be in the mouth of such a one? It will hardly be said, that this madman had been under the hands of either *Jesus* or *Paul*: And how should such a one know, that these *Jews* were impostors; and that the others were not.

It is said, " That before this event St. " *Paul*, for the space of two years, had cured " all sorts of diseases, and ejected demons, in

* Acts xix. 11, 12.

" the

"the name of *Jesus* at *Ephesus*." Granted. "How then, it is farther asked, could this demoniack be ignorant either of *Jesus* or *Paul**?" I answer, that as a demoniack, he very probably had heard of *Paul's* curing of such in the name of *Jesus*; for which very reason the demon who possessed him made the man always avoid St. *Paul*, and would never suffer him to appear in his presence; which plainly was the case, by his continuing in possession of him. But as a madman, if he knew *Paul*, why did not he, in his lucid intervals, apply to him for relief? Or otherwise, why did not his friends do as much for him? which the fame of *Jesus* would the more strongly have impelled them to.

We read in the gospel of one, who did actually cast out devils in the name of *Jesus*, though he was no follower of him; on which account the disciples forbad him; at the same time that *Christ* himself was not displeased at him †. And yet we see how roughly the Jewish exorcists were used by the demoniack, who attempted to cure him in the name of *Jesus*.

* Essay on Demoniacks, p. 277.
† Mark ix. 38. Luke ix. 49.

But

But these cases were very different. The former person, though he had not as yet been received, as a disciple, was in the way to be one. He appears to have had a true faith in Christ, without which he could not have wrought this miracle; and this of course created in him a reverence for Christ and his name; accordingly, being not against them, our Lord reckoned him to be on their part*.

* *He that is not with me is against me,* says Christ, on another occasion, *and he that gathereth not with me, scattereth,* Matt. xii. 30. On the other hand, he here says, *He that is not against us, is on our part, Mark* ix. 40. Luke ix. 50. But here is no contradiction. He that gives no proof of his attachment to me, nor gathers any converts to the religion I teach, I cannot look upon such an one as my friend; but must reckon him to be in an opposite interest. But it is possible, that he who gives me no direct opposition, may in time become a disciple; as he who casts out devils in my name, shews himself to be well inclined towards me, though he has not, as yet, declared himself for me.

He that is not with me, may betray circumstances from which it may be presumed, that he is against me.

And he that is not against me, may discover some inclinations towards me, and be presumed to be for me. These two propositions therefore, which at first sight may seem contradictory, are perfectly consistent with each other.

The above exorcists were professed *Jews*, and only used the name of *Jesus* as a charm, when they could have no faith in him: And therefore they met with such treatment as they deserved, from their abuse of it: Though neither Christ, nor his apostle *Paul*, had any concern in the case.

This was a very publick transaction, and was productive of many great consequences. *It was known to all the Jews, and Greeks also dwelling at Ephesus: And fear fell on them all; and the name of the Lord Jesus was magnified**. The example spread a general terror, whereby men were awed from making too free with the holy name of *Jesus*, the power of which was greatly extolled by these means; and was attended with the conversion of many to the faith. Hence likewise *many of those, who used* curious and magical *arts*, which had a near affinity to exorcisms; and which *Ephesus* was famous for; *brought their books together, and burned them before all men* †; the value of which was computed to amount to no

* Acts xix. 17.
† Ver. 19.

less a sum than *fifty thousand talents of silver**. We see here a great number of real facts, and a real sacrifice, too considerable to be made to a vague opinion.

As counterfeits, when detected, set off the worth of sterling coin; so the defeating and exposing of the attempts of these pretenders, served as a foil to the real dispossessions effected by *Paul*, as well as to those of Christ, and of his true disciples in general. This likewise proved a seasonable warning against impostors; and taught men to distinguish between true and false miracles of this kind. And this being the last account, which we have in Scripture-history of demoniacal possessions, it is added very properly to close the rest.

Let us now look back, and take a general view of these cases; and consider what circumstances they are attended with, and what conclusions arise from them, which affect the question before us, concerning the reality of these possessions.

* Supposing these to have been the Roman silver *Denarii*, they have been calculated to amount to 1614 *l.* 11 *s.* 6 *d.* of our money. But if they were Jewish shekels, as others suppose, they amounted to 5703 *l.* 2 *s.* 6 *d.*

1. We

1. We may, I hope, by this time lay these down as facts, of which, general and particular, we have seen a good number: And they appear to be,

2. Facts of great notoriety. They were not done in a corner. They were generally performed in the presence of multitudes; in cities and places of publick resort: Where all men were amazed at them, and the whole country rang with their fame, which was spread far and wide.

3. They were facts of a very singular nature; very remarkable in themselves; of a distinct kind; and such as attracted the notice of men in an especial manner; and made them the more to be observed and attended to.

4. They were particularly taken notice of, and very narrowly examined by enemies, who never could detect any falsehood or deceit in them; but were forced to confess their reality.

5. A confession of the truth and reality of them was extorted from the devils themselves, who were the subjects of them; and on whom these miracles were wrought, in spite of them, to their regret and utter confusion; and by which they suffered, to

the destruction of their very kingdom. The testimony of enemies is always allowed to carry the greatest weight. The testimony of such enemies must amount to demonstration.

6. These were permanent facts. Many, I might say, all, the cases were very obstinate; and some had been of long continuance. And the cures performed with regard to them were effectual and absolute: So that the maladies, as far as appears, never returned.

7. They were facts of great importance, affecting the bodily and spiritual welfare of all those who were subject to them; and the peace, safety and comfort of their relations, friends, and neighbours, and even of society in general.

8. They were more important still in other respects, and in a higher sense; and in more extensive views. They are eminent proofs of the existence of a world of spirits; which will be more particularly spoken to hereafter.

9. These facts are truly miraculous. They were miracles of a special kind, and very astonishing. They proved themselves such in the face of the world; and spread conviction

viction among all sorts of people far and near.

10. These miracles constitute one special kind of the miraculous evidences of Christianity; which are all to be held sacred and inviolable; and ought to be defended, and strenuously contended for, against those that endeavour to interpret them away, in a light sense, very depreciating of them. Their sterling value, and divine signature are not to be defaced and melted down, into the common mass of other miraculous cures; which they are not to be confounded with; whereby they would be disguised, and in a manner lost.

11. These miraculous cures exceeded all others whatsoever. The objects of all our Saviour's healing miracles, but these, were some bodily distempers or complaints. These extended to the healing of the soul, which was their principal object; and bodily distempers at the same time were often removed by them. Hence they were the more excellent and salutary. The divine power, goodness, and mercy was the more manifested in them. They were double miracles, and of the highest value of all others.

12. These miraculous facts are established upon the highest authority; upon the authority of Christ himself, and his apostles. They were his own acts and deeds; and the deeds of those, who were commissioned by him to perform them. None then durst dispute, or could doubt of the truth and reality of them. They were attested, as just now observed, by the devils themselves, who felt the power of them. And it is strange, that men in these days should have the hardiness to cavil at them; or attempt to give a different turn to them, so as to alter their very nature; and destroy the most valuable and beneficial part of them.

13. The multitude and variety of these facts are likewise very observable; each of which contributes to ascertain the rest: And they all together mutually support each other; and concur in establishing the authenticity of the whole.

14. These miraculous facts were more circumstantially, and more repeatedly recorded; most of them by two, many by three evangelists, than scarce any other miracles, or facts whatsoever in the gospel.

15. These

15. These facts may now plead possession. They have had the sanction of time; and the prescription and establishment of ages. They were entered upon record, in the age they were performed; and even by several persons concerned in them: And it is a known maxim in the law, that records prove themselves. The law likewise allows antient books to be good evidence, with regard to facts that exceed memory. These facts are kept on record, in a very antient book; and have the credit of history to rest upon, in common with all other antient, well-authenticated facts: And it is iniquitous, and perverse, and contrary to all the laws of evidence, and the rules of fair reasoning, to call them in question *.

Let us in the next place, enquire into the character of the historians, who record these facts. These are the four evangelists.

For we have seen one instance of a possession recorded by St. *John*. And it is very observable, that, being more sparing of such relations than the other evangelists,

* See Dr. Worthington's Boyle's Lectures, Disc. iv. p. 119.

it is he expressly, by name, as mentioned by two of them, who informed our Saviour of a man who cast out devils in his name, and was forbidden by him, and some of the other disciples*, out of a jealousy of their master's honour, and their own; lest persons, not commissioned by him, should invade their province in this respect: Where it is plain, that *John* bears witness to this man's having actually cast out devils: Whence it likewise appears, that he reckoned this the peculiar practice and prerogative of Christ, and his apostles. And this, together with his mention of *Satan's* possessing *Judas* †, entitles him to be of the number of the historians, who recorded the accounts of demoniacal possessions.

Now, to consider their qualifications for this undertaking. It might be sufficient to insist upon their being inspired writers, and therefore infallible.

But it will moreover be a satisfaction to all unprejudiced enquirers to find, that these persons had some qualifications, pe-

* Mark ix. 38. Luke ix, 49.
† Jo. xiii, 27,

culiarly

culiarly adapted to their employment of recording these matters.

Two of them were apostles, whom our Lord chose for the special witnesses of his transactions, and of this kind of them among the rest; which of course, therefore, they often, if not always, must have seen him perform. The other two are supposed to have been of the number of his seventy disciples, who often attended him likewise; and had frequent opportunities of observing the cures he performed upon Demoniacks.

They were all commissioned by him to cast out devils themselves; and they executed their commission with success. When they, at one time, returned to him, from a mission on which he had sent them, and made report of the issue of it, *Lord*, said they, *even the devils are subject to us through thy name*.

Now these men must surely have had sufficient experience to qualify them for recording these matters; and for distinguishing between real possessions and feigned, or imaginary ones. They had been eye-witnesses of the many miracles of this kind wrought by Christ. They had been concerned in many themselves.

They

They felt this power within them: And they never failed to exercise it, when they met with objects of it. There is but one instance upon record, in which they failed to eject a malignant spirit out of one possessed by him. But that was not because there was no devil in the man to cast out, but because he had taken a too strong hold, and possession in him, for their abilities to overcome.

And this very obstinacy of his confirmed the reality of the possession. They never had the least doubt about that: And Christ himself having dispossessed him in their presence, he, by this means, ascertained the fact, and set his seal to the truth of it.

These were extraordinary cases; and here were extraordinary qualifications in the persons who were to record them, which put them above all exception.

One of the historians, who recorded these miracles, was yet better qualified for the purpose than the rest. St. *Luke* was a physician *: And he would not have been mentioned as such, had he not been eminent in his profession. He is *the brother,*

* Col. iv. 14.

whose praise is in the gospel, throughout all the churches *. As the care and fidelity of this sacred historian redound to his character in general: So particularly doth his recording of demoniacal cases entitle him to singular esteem and regard; " and his style " and manner of writing are much com- " mended by some of the most learned of " the same profession: Who acknowledge, " that, as a physician, he well understood " the force and meaning of words; and " that his language is more simple, and " correct, as well as more physical, than " that of the other evangelists †."

Now, as St. *Luke* had *perfect understanding of all things from the very first* ‡, and had the best opportunities of informing himself in the several demoniacal cases particularly—As he partook of, and may be supposed to have proved, and exercised the power of ejecting evil spirits himself, being one of the seventy, to whom that power was communicated—As he was, by his

---

* 2 Cor. viii. 18.

† Dr. *Mead*, and Dr. *Freind*, from Dissert. on Demoniacks, p. 37.

‡ Luke i. 3.

profession, well qualified for forming a true judgement upon these cases; and for distinguishing between them and natural disorders—As, besides the cases which he records in his gospel, he gives an account of some others in his *Acts* of the apostles, which lay out of the design of the other evangelists—And as he is so full " and co-" pious, so exact and particular, in record-" ing them all," his authority alone, setting aside his divine inspiration, must surely be admitted as decisive. If, in any of these cases, which he records, he had had any suspicion of their not being real possessions, he would not surely have expressed himself so positively and peremptorily about them; or if there had been any obscurity or ambiguity in his style or diction; whereby criticks might have room to put a different sense upon his words; this would have rendered his evidence doubtful: But as he delivers his testimony concerning possessions, with so much plainness, accuracy, and precision, conformably to the rest of his writings, and to the accounts of the other evangelists; this surely, when duly weighed and considered, must stop the mouths of all gainsayers.

Such

Such is the result of this enquiry—such are the cases which have been the subject of it—such the facts, as they have turned out—and such the witnesses of them! Whence I flatter myself they might safely be left to rest upon their own bottom, without adding any thing more in support of them.

For, upon a review of what hath been said, considering the multitude and variety of the cases; the clearness, precision, and reiterated force of the evidence; the concurrence of so many circumstances; the credit, character, and authority of the witnesses: I do not know what can now be wanting to establish in our minds a full and thorough conviction of them; nor what can *now* be said to invalidate the belief of these possessions.

Notwithstanding, it may be expected, that some notice should be taken of what *hath* been said against the reality of them.

I shall therefore proceed, in the next place, to make a few general remarks upon the grounds and principles of the Essay on Demoniacks, and to obviate such particular objections contained in it, as seem to carry most weight in them.

And

And first I must observe, that the chief principle, on which this Essay is founded, is wrong, erroneous, and absolutely indefensible, in every view of it.

The doctrine of the Essay is, "That "Christ and his evangelists, in speaking "and writing of Demoniacks, always "made use of the popular language of "the age and country, which signified "their being really possessed with de-"mons, agreeably to the vulgar notion in "that respect: When yet they themselves, "at the same time, in truth, believed no "such thing; but, on the contrary, looked "upon those possessions, as being only fan-"ciful and imaginary."

This I take to be the purport of the main doctrine of the Essay; and the principle on which it is built, and which runs through it, can be none other than this, or to this effect — "That it is allowable to pro-"fess one thing, and believe the con-"trary: And that it is justifiable for "men, in their words and actions, and "in their whole outward conduct, to "proceed in a manner contradictory to "the convictions of their own minds;
"and

" and that in matters of the most serious na-
" ture; in the great concerns of morality
" and religion."

This principle is not directly avowed in the Essay in so many words. I wish the author had laid down his principles expresly. But it is collected from what occurs frequently in it, and particularly from the whole tenour of chap. II. sect. iii. And I hope is fairly represented; than which I wish nothing more.

Now I maintain, that this principle is false in itself, and injurious in the application; and that it cannot be defended by any known rules of good writing; or any sound maxims of morality whatsoever. For by what laws of interpretation; what canons of criticism; what figure in rhetorick; are any writers to be understood in a sense directly contrary to that in which they express themselves? By none certainly.

The style of the gospel-history, though the work of different writers, is all uniform throughout. It contains the same plain narration of facts in the account which it gives of our Saviour's miracles of all sorts; of his life and death, his resurrection and
ascen-

ascension. But according to this mode of interpretation, the gospel accounts of demoniacks are all to be read backwards: And if this rule is pursued, his other miracles may be interpreted in the same manner. His temptation hath already been represented, as being all visionary; and so may his sufferings and death, his resurrection and ascension, be treated as such likewise: Nor at this rate shall we know when to stop, nor where such *liberties of prophesying* will end.

There were hereticks of old, the *Docetæ*, I think they were called, who held, that *Christ* really did not suffer or die in his own person; but that the man, who was compelled to carry his cross, was substituted in his stead. These hereticks were soon exploded. And indeed I think the opinion contended for is not much less absurd. The principle of it is not only absurd, but pernicious.

There lately was, and still is, in some countries, a society of men who held it lawful to dissemble the truth, and even to lie for it. But I know not of any besides the fraternity of the *Jesuits*, who maintain these detestable maxims.

The

The fastning of any the like imputations upon him, who is truth itself, and upon his true disciples, is the foulest indignity that could be offered them; and the grossest affront to the morality of the gospel. It is shamefully contradicting the numberless historical truths which it relates. It is, in effect, telling the evangelists, that they record untruths; and telling *Christ* himself, that he did not do the things that he assumed to do: Which is shocking to reflect upon.

If such an hypothesis as this were to take place; there would not be a better foundation for the charge of pious frauds, even upon the first founders of our religion. And if our Saviour did cast out devils only in shew, I do not know, how he could be vindicated, if he were accused of being no more than a juggling impostor. A man must have worked himself up to a strange pitch of prejudice, to have the hardiness to withstand such plain declarations of facts; and interpret them all away. I cannot tell, whether the author of the Essay be an occasional conformist, or not. But by the principles which he advances, he makes
Christ

Christ and his evangelists to be excellent ones.

Every author writes to be understood: But there is no understanding of any one, who expresses himself in plain language; which carries an obvious literal sense; and yet hath a covert, latent meaning, of a very different, I may say contrary, nature; which he never discovered to have, nor ever was suspected to have; till at length, after a course of many ages, that discovery is made, with regard to the evangelists; by some that seem to know their meaning better than themselves. It is the greatest abuse of language, thus to be dealt with. If this were permitted; it would be the means of introducing an universal scepticism: And if such liberties are to be taken with the scriptures. we may as well throw our bibles away. Surely, no other book was ever treated in this manner!

The common use of a few terms, relating to speculative matters, which took their rise from a mistaken philosophy; but which do not in the least affect religion or morality; can by no means justify the supposition, that many whole passages in the writings of four different authors carry a signification very different from

from the obvious and literal sense of them. What relation have the vulgar phrases of the *sun's rising*, and *setting*; and the *earth's standing still*, to any revealed truths? Or what effect have they ever had on morality? What analogy have the descriptions of St. *Anthony's* fire, or St. *Vitus's* dance, to the numerous narrations of demoniacal possessions in the gospels? A man must be hard put to it for argument, before he would mention such instances as these, or that of the *night-mare* or *Incubus*, as proofs of our following the customary mode of speaking, without approving the hypothesis*?

But this last instance is an unlucky one for the purpose. With regard to which, the following passage of a philosophical work, well-esteemed, may not be unacceptable to our readers, and is in point.

"Let us consider," says the author, "the disease
" called the *Incubus*, or *night-mare*; which many
" persons are tormented with in their sleep.
" It is generally accompanied with fright-
" ful, ghastly apparitions, which are then
" obtruded upon the imagination; so that
" the party is made to fancy, that the dis-

* See Essay on Demoniacks, p. 316.

" temper

"temper itſelf proceeds from its preſſing
"him down with a weight like to ſtifle
"him. And, for this very reaſon, the
"*Latins* call this diſorder, the *Incubus*; as
"if we ſhould ſay, the *Overwhelmer*, or
"*Oppreſſor:* And the *Greek* name, Εφιαλτης,
"imports much the ſame thing. And
"this, I believe, is allowed to be a caſual
"diſtemper of the brain, by which the
"animal ſpirits are obſtructed.

"But now the bodily indiſpoſition here,
"and the diſagreeable viſion made to ac-
"company it, are *two very different things:*
"And, as it would be abſurd to make the
"diſorder of the material organ, the effi-
"cient cauſe of the apparitions, which are
"exhibited along with it: For theſe are
"often ugly phantoms, which to fright us
"the more, appear to have bad deſigns upon
"us; threaten us; wreſtle with us; get us
"down; all which infer *a deſigning, intelli-*
"*gent cauſe:* So their being exhibited along
"with it, and adapted to it, ſhews us, I
"think, that *theſe beings* wait for, and
"catch the opportunity of the indiſpoſi-
"tion of the body; to repreſent at the ſame
"time

" time something terrifying also to the
" mind*."

From this passage, it appears, that the author of it, thought the *Incubus* to be, not an imaginary, but a real Being, of that sort, the existence of which our Essayist is arguing against.

I have not yet done with the fallacious principle abovementioned. It is highly injurious, in its application to our Saviour, in other respects. It is making him the patron of superstition. True religion is placed in the middle, between the extremes of infidelity, on the one side, and superstition, on the other; equally distant, and averse from both. If the notion of possessions be false and imaginary, the belief of them is superstitious.

It begets in people false fears, and makes them fear, where no fear is. It makes them truely and literally Δεισιδαιμονες. It is raising their apprehensions of Beings that have no power to hurt them; and filling

---

* See an Essay on the Phænomenon of Dreaming; in an Enquiry into the Nature of the Human Soul, Vol. II. p. 140.

them with a dread of such, as have no existence.

It is withdrawing their religious thoughts from the proper object of them; and placing religion where it ought not to be; and on things that do not belong to it. And this, I take to be the true notion and nature of formal superstition.

Now to suppose our blessed Lord, and his apostles, capable of giving any countenance to such superstition—to suppose that he, who came from heaven on purpose to teach pure and undefiled religion, divested from all those lesser superstitious rites and customs, which had crept into the Jewish church; should at the same time countenance, and confirm them, in this gross and flagrant superstition, if it be one—should both by word and deed, propagate it. —should take pains for this purpose—should *go about*, not, as it is said of him, *healing all that were oppressed of the devil*, but only pretending to heal them — This is the height of impiety to conceive: It is diametrically opposite to the gracious design of our Saviour, and to these his wondrous works. If the notion of possessing demons and spirits was surperstitious, it was riveting

ing those notions in the minds of men to all intents and purposes; instead of extirpating them; as he certainly would have done, had they been false and groundless.

We are told, that it doth not appear, that Christ and his apostles had any divine warrant to change the vulgar language, in describing the case of the demoniacks*. They certainly had not. There was no occasion for it. It was the proper language adapted to the truth of things: Otherwise they undoubtedly would have changed it, whether they had had an express warrant, or not. The necessity of the case would have required it.

This writer, while he is combating the doctrine of demoniacal possessions, as being superstitious, is at the same time endeavouring to explain Δεισιδαιμονεςερϒς, the proper term for being too superstitious, into a very different, and much more favourable sense: And compliments St. *Paul* for his politeness, as he would have it, in addressing the *Athenians*; by making him call them *very devout towards demons, or gods* †: In-

---

* Essay on Demoniacks, p. 358.
† Ibid. p. 208.

stead of taxing them *in so shocking a manner*, as we translate it, with being *too superstitious*. For which yet we think he had good grounds, when he saw such proofs of it, in the multitude of heathen altars and images, with which their city abounded. He had otherwise been very unfit for the office of a preacher of the gospel.

Though we are told, that the word Δεισιδαιμων is capable of a good sense: Yet it can never be so understood by Christians, on account of the term Δαιμων; to the worship of which it refers, so incompatible with that of Christians: And its being used by the apostle in the comparative degree would otherwise determine it to a bad sense. To be too religious, which is the most favourable translation it can bear, is to be superstitious. Δεισιδαιμονια was well explained by an antient Etymologist, as being taken by the heathens in a good sense; but that, among Christians, it was put for impiety *.

* Ιςεον, ὁτι παρα μεν Ἑλλησι, επι καλῳ λαμβανεται (Δεισιδαιμων) παρα δε ἡμιν Χριςιανοις επι της ασεβειας λεγεται. Suicer. in voce. Ham. in loc.

The denying of diabolical poffeffions ftrikes at the whole œconomy of revealed religion; of which the reality of thefe poffeffions is a part, and a very confiderable part too; as will appear, when we come to take a view of the true fcripture-demonology, in oppofition to that of the Effay. To proceed,

We are told, " That the fpirits, which " were thought to take poffeffion of mens " bodies, are called in the New Teftament *demons*, not *devils*."— " That by " demons we are to underftand the pagan " deities; and thefe fuch human fpirits, as " fuperftition deified*." Now, as thefe were judged capable of entering the bodies of mankind; I would fain know, where the difference lyes, with regard to the argument, between fuch poffeffions, and poffeffions by other evil fpirits: For evil fpirits they muft have been, of fome fort or other; from their evil operations in thofe whom they poffeffed.

'If any evil fpirits at all might be fuppofed to have entered men's bodies, befides

* Effay on Demoniacks, p. 12. 22.
† Ibid. p. 22.

their own souls, it is of no signification, what the nature, or kind of those spirits was—whether they were the souls of men, or fallen angels. Our opinion concerning them, or even our knowledge of them, could we attain it, makes no alteration in the nature of the case. The *phænomenon* is much the same; and the miracle of ejecting the one, or the other, would be the same likewise.

But this will be considered more particularly hereafter.

In the mean time, let us proceed to another general observation, That, as this performance is faulty in its main principle; so it is in its very foundation. There is no building without a foundation: But this work is raised without any foundation, as far as I can perceive, having been previously laid for it; or, at best, with a very sandy one. It is built upon supposition; taking that for granted, which should have been proved beforehand. What we first meet with to this purpose is a promise, in the contents, of shewing, who first invented the doctrine of possession; as if this was no more than a creature of man's invention, without having any other foundation.

tion. In discharge of this promise, in the place referred to, which is not till we are got a good way into the book, no particular author, or authors, of this doctrine are named, and proved to have been the first broachers of it; but we are only told in general, "That those who first in-"vented this doctrine were men unac-"quainted with nature; and yet ambitious "of accounting for its most mysterious "*phænomena* *:" which we are to take the learned writer's word for.

At the same time, his promise of shewing by whom this doctrine was rejected is punctually performed; and "the sects and "persons, whose minds were not disturbed "by superstitious terrors," and who denied the reality of demoniacal possessions, are expresly mentioned; at the head of whom he is not ashamed to place the *Epicureans* among the heathens, and the *Sadducees* among the Jews †. This doctrine then

* See Essay on Demoniacks, p. 153. Here I cannot help observing, once for all, that there is often more in the contents, than in the body of this book; and that more is promised, than is performed in it.

† Ibid. p. 155.

must

must have obtained, before it could have been rejected.

It is here to be observed farther, that the doctrine of demoniacal possession is a positive one, and built upon facts, as we have seen at large: The denial of it, on the contrary, is of a negative nature, and is a denial of those facts. It is not therefore to be wondered at, that no direct attempt was made to disprove the former, or to prove the latter; because of the impracticability of the thing.

Facts are allowed to be the most obstinate things in the world, and the most difficult to be contended with: And negatives are the hardest of all things to be proved. And whoever undertakes this task in the present case, will have the proving of the negative; both in general, and with regard to every one of the facts particularly; together with the circumstances of each. And how this is to be done, I profess, I am at a loss to guess. This side of the question is capable of no positive proof whatsoever. These facts cannot be disproved by any argument *a priori*; nor by any direct argument at all. It is not enough to say, that the language, in which we have the recital of these facts, was the popular language of the age, in compliance with which it was used, concerning the notion of possessions; and that this notion was a vulgar error: But you must first prove it to be an error. This hath not been done: Nor do I conceive how it can be done. There are but two ways for proving any thing; these, in the language of the schools, are *a priori*, and *a posteriori*. There are no *data* for proving this to be an error, that can be fetched *a priori*. This proof therefore must be set about *a posteriori*. And this can be done no otherwise than by disproving the facts, on which this notion is founded; and which appear in its support.

That the notion of demoniacal possessions had long obtained before our Saviour's time, and continued to prevail in his time, is readily granted; and thanks are due to the learned author for the pains which he hath taken to bring together many proofs of it*: To which some more will be added in the proper place.

The demoniacal possessions and dispossessions in the gospels are so many facts, which

---

* See Essay on Demoniacks, p. 124.

confirm

confirm the truth of this notion. Therefore, before it can be disproved, the facts must be disproved. These lye in the way, and must first be combated. These are its outworks; and if they cannot be demolished, the citadel is impregnable, and the doctrine safe.

Before any argument can be drawn from the conformity of the gospel language, in this respect, to the popular language, grounded upon the notions of the vulgar, which you suppose to have been erroneous; you must farther prove, that Christ, and his evangelists, did not think as they spake, and wrote. You must justify them, in that respect, from the like manner of speaking, and writing, used by them, on other occasions; which, from what hath been said under the last head, can never be done.

You must produce some passages out of Scripture, relating to other subjects, if not to this, wherein the like stile is used; and the like conduct observed. If you cannot do this, you should at least produce something similar, or analogous to it; out of some other grave authors of antiquity, wherein they mention diabolical possessions, as real; but yet discover, by some means or other,

other, that they themselves did in truth believe them to be only imaginary. Nay, do but produce any one paſſage, or ſentence, out of any writer, antient or modern, good, bad, or indifferent, I do not know whether writers of romances need to be excepted, who is not to be underſtood, as he writes; and you will have ſomething to keep you in countenance. But theſe are difficulties not to be ſurmounted.

What other topick can be thought of to help out this argument, I am at a loſs to gueſs, unleſs recourſe be had to Mr. *Hume's* argument of experience. And that argument, I imagine, is by this time ſufficiently exploded. This, however, is at beſt but a negative experience; and therefore a negative proof. It is but your own experience; which extends but a little way. You can only ſay, you never ſaw any demoniacal poſſeſſions; you cannot ſay, other people never did. You do not know what experience thoſe of antient times had to the contrary: Nor, I preſume, have you made any diſcoveries relating to the world of ſpirits, which they were ignorant of. Some teſtimonies, in proof of poſſeſſions, will be produced, in the Appendix, from later times. Their experience was founded on facts. You have no facts to ground any experience upon. Your experience therefore is indeed no experience at all.

Reason is supposed to have no small weight in determining upon the case: Whence we are told, "that there is no suffi-
"cient evidence from reason, for the reality
"of demoniacal possessions: Nay, that reason
"strongly remonstrates against it *."

But what doth reason know of the matter? It is quite out of its province; and is no more an object of it, than musick is to the deaf, or colours to the blind.

Our reason, in its most improved state, considered merely as such, is pressed down to earth, and hardly sees the things before it. The immaterial world is beyond its sphere; and the greatest philosopher knows no more of it, by the help of his reason, than the most ignorant peasant. Our metaphysicks extend but a little way; and that science, if it may be called one, labours under great imperfection and uncertainty.
"Natural theology is in itself a poor,
"weak thing; and reason, unassisted, hath
"not been able to carry the clearest philoso-

---

* Essay on Demoniacks, sect. ix. prop. ix. p. 150.

"phers

"phers very far, in their pursuit after di-
"vine matters*." It is from revelation
alone, that we draw any certain knowledge in this respect. And it is no sign of
a good cause, that men fly from it; and
appeal to that which is so poor a judge of
the matter.

An objection is started towards the close
of the work before us, which, if it hath
any weight in it, ought to have appeared
in its front; as it would then have gone
near to cut the question short, and prevent
any controversy about it.

The objection is, "That the ejection of
"demons is not an object of sight; and
"that it doth not fall within the notice of
"any of the senses †." Whence we are
left to infer, that it cannot properly be the
subject of testimony: And if so, the evangelists were very idle, in attempting to give
any testimony concerning it, and little regard is due to their testimony, however
well it may seem to be authenticated.

But though these incorporeal Beings are
not visible to our fleshly eyes; yet their pos-

---

* *Baker's* Reflections on Learning, chap. ix. Of Metaphysicks.
† *Essay* on Demoniacks, p. 391.

session of men, and their dispossession, might have been visible enough in their effects and consequences; as all those recorded by the evangelists, notoriously were.

There are many *phænomena* in the material world which escape our senses; the reality of which, notwithstanding, is incontrovertible. We cannot see the wind: But we hear the sound of it, and feel its power; which is often very great, though *we cannot tell whence it cometh, nor whither it goeth*.

And this is made use of by our Saviour, as a comparison to illustrate spiritual matters by: And if we are to believe nothing about spiritual Beings, but what falls under our senses; we must not believe so much as the existence of any of them.

It is allowed, that we may know, when a disease is cured: But it is asked, " What " evidence there is, that a *demon* is expelled, " arising from the work itself*?"

To which we may answer, just as much as there is from the cure of a disease; the alteration produced being no less discernible in the one, than in the other; whatever

* Essay on Demoniacks, p. 391.

more,

more. The more violent the paroxysms, in either case, the greater the evidence is, which arises from the total removal of them; be the case what it will: And no natural distemper could ever be attended with more dreadful agonies, than these possessions were; nor any more effectually removed. The variety of the symptoms likewise in these several cases made the cure of them all the more conspicuous.

One would be apt to think, that the man, who started such objections, had never read the gospel-accounts of Demoniacks.

To call these *invisible miracles*—to assert, that they *do not*, and " *cannot furnish any sensible, and publick proofs of Christ's power over demons;*" or " *any proof at all to unbelievers*"—and " *that no miracle of this kind could be a publick display of Christ's power; or a visible victory over the devil; and a sensible manifestation of the glories of his conqueror* *"—and that these were no miracles at all to mankind.—These are downright assertions against fact; as abundantly appears from what hath been already ob-

---

* Essay on Demoniacks, p. 393. 395. 398.

served, and do not deserve any notice to be taken of them.

Were those miracles invisible, which produced such amazement, and were so astonishing to multitudes? What more publick and visible display of Christ's power—what more visible victory over the devil—or more sensible manifestation of the glories of his conqueror, can any reasonable believer, or unbeliever, desire, than such as arose from the confession of the devils themselves?—From the dread and confusion, which they betrayed at Christ's presence? And from their instantly quitting possession, at a word spoken by him, though with the **utmost reluctance?**

The demons were literally incorporated with the demoniacks; and by that means the miraculous dispossessions of them became objects of sense; and the miracle wrought on the one, was wrought on the other too.

The miracles of Christ in general were publick testimonies which God gave to the truth of his mission.—They were the immediate great evidences of the religion he taught; and were wrought for the conviction and conversion of the world to him.

The

The miracles wrought on the demoniacks bear these characters, and answer this intent, as much as healing the sick, or any others; whatever more. Many believed in consequence of them. The patients themselves believed of course: Of whom, some gave express proofs; as, for instance,

The man out of whom the legion was cast: The *Syro-phœnician* woman, and her daughter: And *Mary Magdalene,* who became a zealous disciple, as well as sincere penitent. Can it be supposed, that the wonder of multitudes at these strange works ended in a stupid astonishment? And that it left no lasting impressions upon them? When they asked, *What thing is this? What new doctrine is this?* which these works were performed in attestation of; did not their curiosity carry them to get some farther information concerning it? When they observed, that *with authority he commanded even the unclean spirits,* and *they obeyed* him; did this produce no obedience, no converts among the spectators? When his fame made such a rapid progress, that it immediately *spread abroad throughout all the region round about Galilee**; did it produce no fruits?

* Mark i. 27, 28.

When the man out of whom the legion was expelled, declared throughout all *Decapolis*, what great things Chrift had done for him, to the aftonifhment of all; did he make no converts, even among an irreligious people *? In what fenfe did the feventy fay, that the devils were fubject to

---

* Not long after this, Chrift had occafion to pafs *through the midft of the coafts of Decapolis*. He now found the behaviour of the inhabitants towards him much changed. They defired him to *put his hand upon a deaf man*, who had likewife an impediment in his fpeech, in confidence of a cure. As they had before befought him to depart out of their coafts; now that he returned thither, to avoid giving them any umbrage, he wrought the miracle in fuch a manner, as to have the leaft appearance of a miracle in it. He took the man *afide from the multitude*, that had gathered about him; made ufe of fome means for his cure, though of not much efficacy in themfelves; and having performed it, enjoined filence about it. But in vain: For *the more he charged them, fo much the more a great deal they publifhed it; and were above meafure aftonifhed, faying, He hath done all things well: He maketh both the deaf to hear, and the dumb to fpeak.*

Grotius and *Whitby* fuppofe thefe people were apoftates from *Judaifm:* fome antients reckon them to have been downright atheifts. How impious foever they were; their former rudenefs towards Chrift was now turned into admiration, and of courfe converfion likewife; as is intimated above, p. 31.

them? With reference to what did Christ say, *I beheld Satan, like lightning, fall from heaven?*

With regard to what, did he give his disciples power to tread on serpents, and scorpions; and over all the power of the enemy? To whom, and to what enemy, doth he in all these several places refer; but to this enemy, the devil, and his accursed crew of fallen angels? Whom Christ, and his disciples, vanquished, and triumphed over openly; by thus expelling them out of the bodies of men, as a visible demonstration of the approaching downfal of Satan's kingdom.

Paul and *Silas* having been cast into prison, for ejecting the spirit of divination out of the *Pythoness*; when the prison-doors were miraculously opened by an earthquake, and the bands of all the prisoners were loosed; on this divine attestation to the reality of the dispossession, the jaylor in consternation asked, what he must do to be saved? Whereupon he, and his family, on hearing the Word of the Lord preached to them, were *straightway baptized, believing in God, with all his house* *.

* Acts xvi. 16.

Now here was a complicated miracle, which was powerfully felt; and which affected all men's senses, wrought in confirmation of such a one, as is styled an *invisible one*; and which was productive of the conversion of a whole family to the faith of Christ.

When the evil spirit prevailed over the Jewish exorcists, and at the same time acknowledged the power of Jesus, and *Paul*; *fear fell on all them that dwelt at Ephesus; The name of the Lord Jesus was magnified: Many believed, confessed, and shewed their deeds: Many also which used curious arts, publickly burned their books, and the word of God mightily grew and prevailed**.

What was the cause of all this so general an alteration in men's religious sentiments and practices?

Not the evil spirit's prevailing over the *Jewish* exorcists only; but his acknowledging the superior power of *Jesus*, in conjunction with that of *Paul*; who had lately given such signal proofs of it.

Were all these " works totally hid " from human view †?" Were they quite

---

* Acts xix. 17—20.
† Essay on Demoniacks, p. 393. 395.

" indis-

indiscernible by mankind? And quite un-
" supported by any evidence, arising from
" the works themselves?" These are such
glaring contradictions to the truth of facts,
so disparaging to our Saviour's miracles, so
derogating from the share which they had,
to a great degree, in the propagation of the
gospel, as do better become unbelievers,
into whose mouths they are put, than any
sincere Christian.

After these general observations, let us
now descend to the consideration of some
particulars; which will bring us to the
critical part of this work, on which it
chiefly hinges?

And here we are, in the first place, told,
" that the spirits, which were thought to
" take possession of men's bodies, are, uni-
" formly, and invariably, called in the
" New Testament, *demons*, and not devils"
" —That by demons, we are to understand
" the pagan deities—and these such human
" spirits as superstition hath deified—that
" the devil is here out of the question, hav-
" ing nothing to do with possessions:" And
that " the word, which in our translation
" is rendered *devils*, ought to be rendered
" *demons*." All this is expressed or implied,

in the first and second propositions of this work.

Now, if it be made appear, that *demon*, in the original, is a name belonging to the devil; and given to him by heathen writers of good authority, the simple use of it in possessions cannot be understood as absolutely exclusive of him: And if there are any instances in the New Testament of the devil's possessing men under any other name, than that of demon, this breaks the uniformity of possessing spirits being called demons, and he must be allowed not to be wholly unconcerned in possessions: Likewise, if any other spirits can be proved to enter men's bodies, besides the spirits of deified mortals; and especially, if it can be made out, that no human spirits, however they may have been thought to be the possessing demons, ever really did take possession of any other men's bodies, at the same time, supposing the reality of these possessions—if these several points can be satisfactorily made good: The foregoing positions all fall to the ground, and our English translation, in this respect, is justified.

First,

First, I am to shew, that Δαιμων is a name belonging to the devil, and given to him by antient heathen writers, of good authority.

In the opposition of the good and evil principles, mentioned by *Plutarch*, the good principle is called Θεος, and the evil principle Δαιμων*; as it were κατ' εξοχην; than which no better proof can be given of the devil's title to this name, and that by original prescription, before there existed any other Being, to whom it might be applicable; the tradition concerning an evil principle having undoubtedly originated from him, as being the author of all evil, natural and moral. *Plutarch*, in his *Dio*, informs us, that this tradition of an evil principle was of so great antiquity, that its first author could not be found; and that it was embraced as truth, by the generality of the wisest heathens: *Diogenes Laertius*, in his account of it, calls the evil principle, κακον δαιμονα. And by *Ocellus Lucanus*, another very antient writer, he is called κακοδαιμων.

* Plutarch. de Iside & Osiride.

We have another very antient authority in *Hermes Trismegistus*, who, with his disciple *Asclepius*, called the devil, δαιμονιαρ-χην, the prince and ruler of demons, agreeably to the scripture-account of him: And these latter he calls αγγελυς πονερυς; who, he says, are the enemies of men, and vex them; and who, on account of their depravity, had been degraded, in plain allusion to the scripture-account likewise *.

Here, I presume, are authorities sufficient to prove the devil's right to the name Δαιμων, which was the first point to be shewn; and that, if we may make use of a term in law, he may be called Δαιμων *paramount*. Some writers in this controversy were not willing to allow, that other evil demons had any thing to do with the evil principle, of which they would fain stop short, in tracing their origin †: But, in this last-mentioned authority, we see their connexion with each other; and that all evil demons were esteemed to be none other

---

* Lact. de orig. erroris, lib. ii. sect. 14, 15.
† Sykes farther enquiry about Demoniacks, p. 20. Review of the controversy about Demoniacks, p. 10.

than fallen angels, long before the gospel appeared in the world.

It appears from *Homer*, *Pindar*, and other Greek writers, who lived many ages before Christ, that the opinion of evil demons prevailed among them in very early times; and that they took the office of these wicked Beings to be intirely of the same nature with that assigned to the devil, and his angels, in Scripture; and consequently it is highly probable, that they were the same implacable and malicious Beings.

Before we proceed any farther, it will be proper, according to the method above laid down, just to point out some instances from scripture of the devil's personal possession of men. It hath been already shewn, that he himself, by his names, *Satan* and *Beelzebub*, was concerned in possessions*. We have seen likewise, that the devil, by both his names, διαϐολος, and *Satan* entered into the body of the traitor†. And because some pains have been taken to persuade us, that *Satan* is not the devil's proper name; it

* P. 61.
† P. 91.

may not be amiss here to subjoin to what hath been advanced above in opposition to that notion, that שטן *Satan*, in the old testament, is by the LXX translated διαβολος, no less than seventeen times.

To proceed, it was the devil himself, by this his proper name, *Satan*, and no inferior *demon*, or evil spirit, who bowed together, and bound a poor woman for eighteen years; as observed above*. We said besides, That *Jesus went about doing good, and healing all that were oppressed of the devil*†. Where his doing good, I apprehend, is to be understood in a general sense; but more especially of his healing bodily diseases, as he had not the means of doing much good otherwise.—And his healing all that were oppressed of the devil, is particularly, and by way of distinction, to be understood of his casting out *the devil*. This I take to be the primary sense at least of this passage, as well as the most obvious. For though many may, and, I fear, are too much in the power of the devil, without being bodily possessed by him, yet those, who

* P. 89.
† Acts x. 38.

were so taken possession of, must have been much more under his dominion, than any others. They must have been, beyond conception by us, who I hope are all safe from this his oppression, overpowered, subjugated, and tyrannized over by him; when, having got possession of them, he tortured and tormented them; had them wholly in his own power; and used it over them, in the most unmerciful manner, that his hellish malice could invent; as is related in the gospel. Surely none could be so much, and so effectually *oppressed*, as those who were *possessed* by the devil.

To say, " That the apostle here refers " to Christ's cure of the deceased in ge- " neral; without taking into consideration " the particular case of the demoniacks [*]," is an unjust representation of his meaning. For doth not he make particular mention of it? The cure of the deceased in general is included in the former member of the sentence, which is expressed in general terms, *he went about doing good*. Dr. *Sykes*' resolution of this passage into Christ's recovering men from the power of the devil,

[*] Essay on Demoniacks, p. 74.

to the obedience of God*, falls far short of the energy of the expression, and is interpreting it away: And even in this general sense, by healing *all* that were oppressed by the devil, he must of course, have healed them that were possessed by him, among the rest; who suffered his oppressions in other respects. It is rightly observed, in opposition to him, that St. *Peter* is here shewing, that Christ's divine commission was demonstrated by his miracles: And we may therefore add, by this miracle of casting out devils, as much as, whatever more than, any others.

The devil is called, *The prince of the power of the air; the spirit that now worketh in the children of disobedience* †. The word in the original for *worketh* is ενεργουντος, which loses much of its force in our translation. Its literal and full signification is, *To work with energy.* The possessed were called Ενεργουμενοι by ecclesiastical writers. It appears therefore from hence, that the devil, or his angels, were those that pos-

---

* Ib. Gr. Ιωμενος παντας τες καταδυναστουμενες υπο τε διαβολε. There is nothing that answers the idea of healing in the above interpretation.

† Eph. ii. 2.

sessed and worked thus powerfully within them.

These scripture proofs are sufficient to shew, that the devil himself was concerned in possessions.

Let us now go on with some more heathen authorities, to prove that possessing demons were not always understood by them to have been the spirits of deified defunct mortals; but that possessions were often attributed by them to spirits of another kind.

Now I would here previously observe, that if the antient heathens were not all unanimous in this persuasion, that demons *always* signified departed souls; and that though some, or even the greater part of them, were of this opinion; yet, if there were others that held there were different kinds of demons; and that some of them were fallen angels; this hypothesis hath not *sufficient* grounds to stand upon. For unless the notion of demons was always and universally restrained by them to the former sense; the assertion, that it was, is false. Nor doth it by any means follow, that the writers of the *new Testament*; supposing them to write in conformity to the style and notions of those

heathens

heathens and *Jews* that lived before them; were confined to that sense likewise: But that they might, and most probably did, as will appear hereafter, by *demons* understand apostate angels, or evil spirits in general; without entering into their specifick natures.

That the antients were much divided in this respect, I might appeal to the learned writer himself. It appears, from the authorities which he hath collected; and particularly from his own observations*; that several philosophers taught, that the heathen *demons*, and I know of no christian ones, he means *demons* in the account of the heathens, were evil spirits of a rank superior to mankind. These we find from him were the principles of some of the learned gentiles; the *magi*; the philosophers; and particularly of *Plato*. These, he says, were the pagan instructors of the fathers; who ascribed to the celestial *demons* whatever the heathens in general attributed to the deified ghosts; and consequently accounted for possessions, without referring them to human spirits. Where he him-

* P. 49. note.

self

self seems to adopt the opinion of the heathens in general, in opposition to that of the philosophers; and the fathers; whose sentiments will be seen hereafter; and " whose " attachment to the gentile philosophy," he says, " led them to represent possessing de- " mons as spirits of a higher order than " mankind."

The fathers are greatly obliged to him: But they had much better instructors than those he is pleased to give them. For the sake of having a gird at them, he hath overshot himself; and while he was endeavouring to shew that they borrowed their notions from the heathen philosophers, he forgot that his own opinion, and the *thesis* he hath laid down, contradicted both the one, and the other: And that instead of the doctrine, which he would fain establish, that *demons* were *always* taken to signify departed souls; he hath made it appear against himself, that the wisest of the antients were of a different opinion; and that he hath only the ignorant vulgar to keep him in countenance. So far is he from having them all unanimously on his side, as they ought to have been, in order to the making of his point good.

M   Indeed

Indeed the heathens in general had no grounds on which to form their notions concerning them; and their speculations about them were all conjecture. Their philosophers had only their own darkened reason at best; by which they could frame any opinion concerning Beings, too subtil for the eye of reason, to have any discernment of; though somewhat assisted perhaps by a wretched experience of their malignity.

Plato, the wisest of them, ingenuously confessed; that the knowledge of them, and of their origin, was above his comprehension *.

However let us see what he, and some of his followers, thought concerning the nature of possessing *demons*. The twelve gods, *majorum gentium*, as they are called, are vulgarly supposed to have been deified mortals: They therefore, according to the doctrine of the Essay, were possessing demons. But these in *Plato's* estimation existed from all eternity †.

According

---

* Περι δε των αλλων δαιμονων ειπειν, και γνωναι την γενεσιν, φησι Πλατων, μειζον η καθ' ημας. Clem. Alex. Strom. lib. v. p. 589. ex Timæo.

† Juno, Vesta, Minerva, Ceres, Diana, Venus, Mars, Mercurius, Jovis, Neptunus, Vulcanus, Apollo.—
Quos

According to *Apuleius*, these were certain middle powers, between the Gods and men; whom the *Greeks* called δαιμονας; and he describes them accordingly: And says, that some of them befriended mankind, and others hated, afflicted, and plagued them; and were enraged at some men; while they soothed and cajoled others*. This is a just description of possessing *demons*.

Porphyry, the great patron of *demons*, as *Eusebius* calls him, describes them in the like manner. He reckons there are some men; whose souls have *demons* always adhering to them; especially at their meals; and that they plague them unmercifully; when they get the better of them—That the prince of them, whom he calls *Sarapis*, *Hecate*, and *Pluto*, supplies charms for expelling them—that these *demons* commit many outrages in their temples—that their *houses* were full of them, and their *bodies* likewise. These *demons* were of an order superior to the souls of mortals. He says farther of them, that their chief delight is

---

Quos deos Plato existimat, neque fine ullo, neque exordio; sed prorsus et retro æviternas. Apuleius de deo Socratis, p. 65.

* Ib. p. 68.

in blood and ordure; which that they might enjoy, they entered the bodies of those that dealt with them.—That they likewise delighted in libations, and certain kinds of meat, which therefore were offered in sacrifice to them; on the steam or *nidor* of which they were supposed to feed; while their votaries feasted upon them*. For, as these *demons* were thought to possess the bodies of those that sacrificed to them; " the
" heathens did not take these to be pure spi-
" rits; but to have grosser vehicles, by which
" they were supposed capable of receiving
" sensible pleasure and benefit by the sacrifi-
" ces: On this account they thought the *ni-*
" *dor* of the sacrifices so suitable to their na-
" tures, especially when themselves had the
" liberty of prescribing them, who best knew
" what was most congruous and agreeable to
" themselves; as that they could insinuate
" themselves into the sacrifices, by means
" of these subtler vehicles; and conse-
" quently convey themselves into the bo-
" dies of their votaries †:" while they feasted on them.

* Porphyry de oraculorum philosophiâ, apud Euseb. præp. evang. lib. iv. cap. 22, 23.
† Dodwell on Schism, chap. xvi. sect. xxiii.

That

That evil spirits took the opportunity of conveying themselves, in some such manner, into men's bodies, while they were at their meals, is greatly confirmed from *Satan's* having entered into *Judas*, as soon as he had received the sop*. It was in allusion to these heathen sacrifices, that St. *Paul* says, *Ye cannot be partakers of the Lord's table, and the table of* Devils †. For so, I hope, we may by this time translate.

Our English translation, in this respect was well vindicated in a discourse from the pulpit some years ago, entitled, " The usu-
" al interpretation of Δαιμονες and Δαιμονια,
" in the New Testament, asserted ‡.

The learned author of a critical dissertation concerning the words Δαιμων and Δαιμονιον hath so ably discussed this point, that I shall take the liberty of subjoining here some of his conclusions; referring to the work itself for his authorities, and the proofs deduced from them.

" From the authorities produced, says
" he, it appears highly probable,

---
* John xiii. 27. 30.
† 1 Cor. x. 2.
‡ Dr. Hutchinson's Sermon, 1738.

"First, That the Greek authors, who preceded the birth of Christ, did not always understand, by the words Δαιμονες and Δαιμονια, the spirits, or ghosts, of departed men; even when these words were applied to finite Beings.

"Secondly, That when they were taken in a bad sense, they were generally supposed to mean such Beings, as the apostate Angels are represented to be in scripture; since the office, and disposition of the apostate angels are attributed to these Beings. And,

"Thirdly, That the *Egyptians, Chaldæans, Phœnicians, Persians, Greeks,* &c. did all firmly believe the existence of one particular evil Being, under whose conduct, and direction, were many others; and that, from what we find delivered by the most antient writers of all these nations; these evil Beings did, in nature, office, and disposition, agree with *the devil, and his angels*; as the sacred writers describe them*."

With regard to the sense, in which the words Δαιμονες and Δαιμονια are used in the *New Testament*, he deduces the following observations,

* Crit. differt. p. 17.

" 1. The

"1. The antient *Greek* authors, who preceded the birth of Christ, seem to have annexed the same idea to the word Δαι-μων and Δαιμονιον, when taken in a bad sense, as the evangelists did in the *New Testament*.

"2. If it could be proved, that two different ideas were annexed to this word by sacred and profane authors, yet this would not affect the present controversy concerning the meaning of *Demoniacks* in the *New Testament*; which must be determined by the true sense and meaning of the word Δαιμων, or Δαιμονιον, in the *evangelists*.

"3. In the *evangelists*, the word Δαιμων, or Δαιμονιον, always denotes an intelligent Being, of a most malignant, noxious, and accursed nature.

"4. The Devil himself is here placed at the head of these Beings: They are here represented to be entirely of his nature and disposition; to have in common with him, the name Δαιμων, or Δαιμονιον; and to act in subserviency to him: And such Beings as these are moreover in scripture called his *angels*, that is, *fallen angels*.

" The Demons therefore in the *New Tes-*
" *tament*, are *fallen angels.*

" 5. Those unfortunate wretches, who
" are called *Demoniacks* by the evangelists,
" were really and truly possessed by these
" accursed spirits; who brought upon them
" those diseases, which, in the gospels, they
" are said to have been afflicted with *."

We have here seen such positive proofs from heathen and sacred writers, that possessing *demons* were spirits of a very different nature from, and superior to, human souls, as may be thought sufficient to determine this controversy: But I am willing to follow our author a little farther; and to examine, in a more direct manner, the position which he lays down, in his second proposition, " That by possessing demons, " in scripture, and elsewhere, are to be " understood such of the Pagan deities, as " had once been men."

But here, before we proceed farther, I would fain know, that supposing them such, where the difference would lye, with regard to the argument, between such possessions, and possessions by any other evil spirits. For evil spirits they must have been, of some

* Ibid. p. 26.

sort

sort, or other, from their evil and mischievous treatment of those, whom they possessed: And the dispossessing, of the one, or the other, would make no difference in the nature of the miracle: It being of little signification, with regard to the question before us, what the nature or kind of those spirits was—Whether they were the souls of men, or fallen angels. Our opinion concerning them, or even our knowledge of them, could we attain it, would make no difference in the nature of the case. The *phænomenon* would be much the same, and the miracle of ejecting the one, or the other, would be the same likewise.

But now to the question, " Whether by " possessing *demons*, we are to understand " the pagan deities; and those such human " spirits, as superstition hath deified." That the heathens paid divine honours to deceased mortals, is readily acknowledged. These were generally their heroes, and kings, and great conquerors, who had been, by their invention of useful arts, or the good they did, benefactors to mankind; or else, by the atchievements which they performed, admired by them. And these they reckoned *demons*.

Pytha-

Pythagoras, according to his commentator, understood these *demons*, in a good sense, of the souls of virtuous men: But at the same time he takes care to distinguish them from such as were των φυσει δαιμονων, *demons* by nature: And he reckons them, ισοδαιμονες, and ισ-αγγελυς. They could therefore be no more *demons* in reality, than they could be really angels*. They were advanced for their virtuous deeds, to be *demons* and gods of an inferior rank, and supposed to be propitious to mankind: These therefore could not be such *demons* as entered the bodies of men, and tormented them so cruelly as is described. This is characteristical of *demons* of a contrary nature. For that there were good and bad *demons* was generally held by the heathens. And *Plato* observes, in this respect, that as heat cannot chill, nor cold burn; so no hurt can accrue from good *demons*, nor any good proceed from wicked ones †. Possessing spirits must have a malignancy superior to that of the wickedest mortal that ever existed: And if they once were mortals, they must be converted into very devils.

---

* Hierocles in Aurea Carm. Pythag.
† Porphyry ubi supra.

And

And if we give ourselves but a moment's time to reflect, we must be fully convinced; that to imagine the souls of men defunct, and absolutely deprived of their own bodies, could have any power, or desire, of entering into the bodies of other men, living or dead, is such an absurdity, as is contrary to all rational, and natural principles whatsoever; and to all the *phænomena* of nature. If they could have entered any bodies, it is more natural to think, they would have re-entered their own; rather than that they would attempt to gain admission into such as were pre-occupied by the souls to which they were at first united.

Apollo, as *Celsus* writes, advised the *Metapontines* to worship *Aristeas*, as a god. They, being satisfied that *Aristeas* was a mere mortal, and perhaps not a very good one, would not, in so glaring a case, believe the oracle that he was a god, or worthy of divine honour: And therefore, maugre the commands of the deity, nobody acknowledged *Aristeas* for a god [*]. And if the god of wisdom had endeavoured to persuade them, that *Aristeas* was a possessing *demon*; I doubt not, but this sensible people would have paid the same regard to his sage advice.

[*] Origen. contra Celsum, lib. iii. p. 128.

Well

Well therefore might the author of the Essay, when he had changed the question, assert, "That it hath never yet been proved from reason, that the spirits of dead men have power to enter, and torment the living—to govern their bodily organs, in as perfect a manner, as their own souls can do—to deprive them of their understandings; and to render them blind, deaf, and dumb. Reason shews us, that they have no such power *."

I readily subscribe to him. Notwithstanding this, certain it is, that though the best and wisest of the antient philosophers taught, that the *demons* in general were evil spirits of a rank superior to mankind, as is acknowledged by our author; yet the vulgar for the most part ran into an opinion, that they were only the spirits of deceased mortals, who were concerned in possessions; and some of name were carried into a persuasion of it. *Josephus* is generally supposed to have been of this opinion, though this hath been disputed: † And *Justin M.* is pressed into it; but I think wrongfully, as will appear hereafter.

* Essay, p. 150.
† See *Twell's* answer to *Sykes's* enquiry, p. 6.

But the question is not, What the heathens, and this, or that man, of any other denomination, thought of *demons*; or in what sense they understood them, or their usurped office, of possessing the bodies of men; but in what sense the scripture takes, and represents them. The inspired writers were not to be taught by the unenlightened heathens; what they were to think of divine and spiritual matters of any kind; especially of the nature of Beings, which were so much out of their ken; and which they had but very obscure notions of at best.

Much less was he, who was the light of the world, to learn from them, who lived in darkness; whose errors he came to remove, and whose false notions, in this very respect, it was his gracious purpose to correct. He, who was to turn men from darkness to light, and from the power of *Satan* to God, would have acted directly opposite to his mission; if he had acted, or expressed himself, in such a manner, as to confirm, or countenance them, in their false opinions of *Satan*, and his accursed crew of wicked spirits. Thus to represent him doth in some measure resemble the charge of the *Pharisees* themselves; that he was in confederacy with

with *Satan*. He came to overthrow the kingdom of *Satan*; and to dethrone all those *principalities* and *powers*, of which it was constituted; and all those *rulers of darkness*, and wicked spirits; who were subject, and subservient to him. This kingdom *Satan* had set up over mankind; whereby, among other bad fruits of it, *they became vain in their imaginations, and their foolish heart was darkned* *.

In order therefore to overthrow this kingdom, it was requisite to enlighten their hearts, and understandings; and to give them some knowledge of these their spiritual enemies; and of their nature. To open their eyes; and let them see, what formidable adversaries they had to encounter; and against whom they could not hope to prevail; if they were suffered to continue in ignorance of them. This our Saviour was not wanting in providing against. He sent his Spirit to guide his Apostles into all truth: And he particularly endowed them with the faculty of *discerning spirits* †. And his beloved disciple exhorts them, *not to believe every spirit*; but *to try the spirits,*

* Rom. i. 21.
† 1 Cor. xii. 10.

whether they are of God; because there were some spirits, that *were not of God**. We have frequent warnings of the devil, and his angels: And can we think that the *demons*, which we likewise read so much of, were none of them?—That they had no relation to *Satan*; and made no part of his retainers? Why did our Lord make it so much his business to cast them out of men's bodies, wherever he met with them? Was all this done in empty shew? Was there no truth, or reality in it? Had it no meaning? Were these *demons* all this while no *demons*; but *mere fictions of the human imagination*, and down-right *non-entities*? For as such they have been represented. What kind of part is this, which we give our Saviour to act, on such a supposition? Is it in the least degree worthy of him; of his character; or the dignity of his person? Is it worthy, or conceivable of any man of common sense, conduct, or character, whatsoever?

What could be more suitable to Christ's undertaking to dethrone *Satan*, and overthrow his kingdom; than to begin his work with the destruction of this his forlorn hope; the expulsion of these his members?

---

* 1 Jo. iv. 1. 3.

bers? Or, what more agreeable to the general intent of his miſſion, to redeem mankind from their thraldom and ſlavery under the dominion of *Satan*, and to reſtore them to the glorious liberty of the ſons of God? *For this purpoſe the Son of God was manifeſted, that he might deſtroy the works of the devil.* What works of his more manifeſtly ſuch, than theſe diabolical poſſeſſions? And wherein was the Son of God more manifeſted, while on earth, than by thoſe ſignal miracles, which he wrought in difpoſſeſſing the devil, and his angels; the effects of which were ſo conſpicuous?

The ſecond propoſition in this work is, " That by *demons*, whenever the word oc-
" curs in reference to poſſeſſions, either in
" the ſcriptures, or other antient writings,
" we are to underſtand, not fallen angels,
" but the pagan deities; ſuch of them as
" had once been men *."

The reverſe of this hath been ſhewn, with regard to Pagan authors of antiquity †; we are to conſider it, as it relates to ſcripture. Whatever is advanced, as ſcripture, ought

* P. 21.
† P. 186.

to be proved from scripture. To make good this proposition with regard to scripture, it should be proved that whenever the word to be translated *demon*, according to this author, occurs in scripture, in reference to possessions; we are never to understand fallen angels, but always Pagan deities, which had once been men. This ought to be proved in every instance; for it includes all: Or at least, it should be proved in so many, that from thence it may be fairly inferred, it is every where so to be understood.

The learned writer acknowledges, that this word occurs in the New Testament above fifty times, in reference to possessions*. It occurs much oftener †. These instances, however, are enough to pick and choose out of: And if demons always signify departed souls, it would surely be an easy matter to point out some of the places, in which they clearly appear to bear that signification, in respect to possessions. But I see

---

* P. 208.

† The word is used, in itself, or its relatives, in the abstract, or concrete, sixty-nine times, in reference to possessions.

nothing of this done *: And I am pretty confident it is what cannot be done: Nay I defy any man to single out any one text among all these, in which, by any force of criticism, or any shadow of scripture argument, he can make it in the least probable, that by either of the words, Δαιμων or Δαιμονιον, is signified the soul of a departed man, and not a spirit of a different kind; when used with regard to possessions. If this cannot be done, why is the authority of scripture claimed for a doctrine, which cannot be proved from it; and which, I am satisfied, hath no foundation in it? Much hath been said in favour of *Beelzebub*, and in opposition to his being the same with the devil, " That " he was a heathen demon, or deity," and as such, was no other than a deified human spirit; whence it is justly concluded, that

* If we take the learned writer's word for it, he tells you, that " he hath shewn, when used in this con-" nection, by the sacred writers, as well as others, it " constantly denotes a human ghost." Ib. p. 208. But turn to the places which he refers to, and you meet with nothing that comes up to the point. Instead of that he tells you in one of these places, that the sacred writers have not particularly explained the sense, in which they used the word *demon*. With regard to which, more hereafter.

" if

" if the prince of the demons was of human
" extract; no doubt his subjects were so like-
" wise *."

On the other hand, it is allowed, that if *Beelzebub* be a fallen angel, demons, without doubt, are spirits of the same order †." But, as much as this point hath been laboured, the proofs of it are all drawn from heathen and *Jewish* writers; and not so much as a single text of scripture hath been produced in support of it. I need not here repeat what hath been already shewn from scripture §, That *Beelzebub* is none other than the devil. And the authority of scripture alone is what this argument is to be determined by, both in itself, and according to the above mentioned proposition.

The learned writer proceeds to " enquire
" in what sense it is most reasonable to un-
" derstand demons, when used in reference
" to possessions, by Christ, and his apos-
" tles ‡."

And here, as already observed, he says,
" The sacred writers have not particularly

* P. 39.
† P. 31.
§ P. 63.
‡ P. 42.

" explained

"explained the sense, in which they use the word *demon* *."

The sense needs no explanation, being sufficiently obvious in itself. No honest enquirer ever failed to find, or even doubted of it. And he *that runs, may read it,* in the characters, which these accursed spirits always bear, wherever any mention is made of them; concerning which more will be said presently. And to obviate every pretence of this kind, we shall hereafter find, in opposition to what is here advanced, that the sense, in which the sacred writers use the word *demon,* is particularly explained in scripture itself.

He observes farther, "That the writers of the New Testament employ this term to describe the heathen gods, and other deified, or beatified human spirits †."

They sometimes indeed use this term to describe the heathen gods, which their worshipers took to be deified or beatified human spirits; but not which they themselves thought to have been such. The artful manner in which the observation is made renders

* P. 43.
† P. 45.

this distinction necessary. I hope the writers of the New Testament were not to borrow their theology from the heathens: Nor doth it follow, that, because St. *Paul* uses the term *demon* to describe such Beings, as the heathens thought to have been deified, or beatified human spirits, he himself *gave heed to those seducing spirits*, and to those *doctrines of demons*, which he condemned, and forewarned christians against. Though this seems to be insinuated; nay even, " from " these premises it is concluded, that by " *demons*, when used in reference to posses- " sions by the writers of the New Testa- " ment, they meaned such human spirits, " as were thought to become *demons* after " death *." But by whom was this thought? Not by the New Testament writers themselves. This durst not be said. It is only another insinuation: Nor can it ever be fairly concluded, from the bare use of the terms, that the writers of the New Testament, who used them, meaned them in a sense, which they never explained themselves to mean; and which, from the whole tenour of their writings, it clearly appears,

* P. 46.

they never did mean. Notwithstanding, it is contended, without any proof, that they meaned as the heathens did. And all that is offered to prove, that possessing spirits are meaned in scripture of the souls of men, is grounded upon this supposition. For before this could be made a good argument, it was necessary to make the inspired writers, not only to speak, but to think, as the heathens did.

We read in scripture of *the spirits in prison* *: But we do not read of any human spirits, released from the prison of the flesh, being suffered to roam at large; and to be made the scourges, and tormentors of living mortals.

We read of *the souls of them that were slain, for the word of God; and for the testimony which they held, being under the altar* †: And of *the souls of them that were beheaded for the witness of Jesus—living and reigning with Christ a thousand years* ‡. But we do not read of any souls possessing other persons bodies; nor of their being turned into *demons* for that purpose.

---

* 1 Pet. iii. 19.
† Rev. vi. 9.
‡ Rev. xx. 4.

Some

Some writers seem to have a great veneration for these *demons*; and are loath to allow the word sometimes bears a bad sense in scripture, and sometimes means evil spirits *. And so much caution is used in speaking of them, that it *seems* no more, than *somewhat probable*, that *demon* is to be taken in a bad sense, in the writings of *Paul*; and it is left somewhat doubtful, whether the term, when applied to possessing *demons*, is used in a good, or bad sense, by the other writers of the New Testament. Pray point out the text, in which it is once used in a good sense.

One of the two places, in which *demons* are allowed to signify evil spirits, is *James* ii. 19. *The devils also believe and tremble*. It was certainly not for their goodness, that they trembled. But if *demons* signify evil spirits, in one, or two, places; why not in more? Why not in all? Shew any places in scripture where they certainly mean good spirits.

St. *James* might know the truth of what he delivered, from his own observation; when he attended his Lord, in casting out

* See Essay on Miracles, p. 207. note.

devils. He was a witness of their confessing him to be the Christ, the son of God, and of the tremors and convulsions, which his presence threw them, and those they possessed, into: And it is not improbable that the apostle here alludes to their *trembling* on these occasions. And from these and the like dreadful effects, which possessions and dispossessions were attended with, the author of the *Essay on Miracles* might have safely ventured to conclude, they were all evil spirits.

Such I maintain them all to have been, without a single exception. I grant Δαιμων was often used by profane authors in a good sense; and sometimes in an indifferent one. Δαιμονιον likewise was sometimes used in a good sense by them; as in the accounts we have of the demon of *Socrates*. The former term occurs but five times in the New Testament; the latter sixty times: But neither the one, nor the other is ever used, but in a bad sense; and they always signify evil spirits.

The only place, where the word is supposed to bear a favourable meaning, is in *Acts* xvii. 18. where we are informed, *That certain philosophers, of the Epicureans and Stoicks,*

icks, encountered Paul: and some said, *What will this babbler say? And other some, he seemeth to be a setter-forth of* ξενων δαιμονιων, *strange Gods: Because he preached unto them,* Jesus, *and the* Resurrection.

These philosophers were heathens, from whom therefore we are not obliged to take the scripture sense of the word, Δαιμων. Notwithstanding I do not see how they can be understood to have used it otherwise than in a bad sense. The terms refer to *Jesus*, it is true. But as all words are to be taken in the sense of those that uttered them: And as these heathen philosophers were but ill disposed towards Christ, and his apostles; they could not have any good meaning in the word, when they applied it to him.

Much is built upon Mr. *Mede's* authority in this controversy; I therefore appeal to it, with regard to the scripture sense of the word Δαιμονιον.

" The word Δαιμονιον, says he, is in the
" scripture never taken in the better, or in-
" different sense, howsoever prophane au-
" thors do so use it; but always in an evil
" sense, for the devil, or an evil spirit *."

* Mede's works, book iii. p. 782.

I shall

I shall therefore venture to resume, that both the words Δαιμων and Δαιμονιον, are always used in the New Testament in a bad sense, of some wicked spirit, or other. But we read of no wicked spirits in scripture, besides the devil and his angels. Nor is there any intimation given, in any part of the sacred writings, of any wicked spirits of a different kind from the devil and his angels. On the contrary, we find them and *demons* often connected together and convertibly used, and predicated of each other. The devil, by his name *Beelzebub* and *Satan*, is called, the prince of *demons*. There is a sameness of character between them. It hath been shewn, that the devil in person, by his name Διαβολος, entered men's bodies, as well as the *demons*. Their entrance, each, was productive of the same kind of symptoms, or effects, in the persons entered by them: Nor could the devil himself have been more mischievous, or tormenting to them, than these *demons* appear to have been. These Beings therefore must be the same, and of the same nature: And *demons* are but another name for devils or fallen angels.

They were generally so understood, by the antients, and moderns likewise; till of late years.

years. In our English bibles, we read devils, instead of *demons*; and it is esteemed a good translation *: And many other versions translate in the same manner; because they are looked upon as synonymous terms. The sacred writers thought they were sufficiently explicit, concerning the nature of these accursed spirits; when they were so repeatedly particular and circumstantial, in describing their bad qualities, and diabolical practices. Scripture however hath condescended to enter into the nature of these *demons* yet farther; and to describe them in such a manner, as that they cannot be understood to have been of human extraction, by any kind of interpretation: But that they must be of a very different nature; even that of the apostate angels; and be intimately connected with the father, and ringleader of all wicked spirits. We read in the *Revelation*;

And I saw three unclean spirits, like frogs, come out of the mouth of the dragon; and out of the mouth of the beast; and out of the mouth of the false prophet. For they are the spirits of devils, working miracles; which go forth to

* See above, p. 174.

the *kings of the earth*; *and of the whole world*; *to gather them to the battle of that great day of God Almighty* *.

This is an emblematical reprefentation of what this divinely-favoured writer faw in a vifion; and his ftyle is accommodated to that of the other infpired penmen; when they treat of the fame fubject. Unclean fpirits are often mentioned in the gofpel, and often called *demons* there: And in one place we read of *a fpirit of an unclean devil* †; parallel to the text before us. And thofe unclean fpirits being here compared to fuch filthy reptiles, as frogs, indicates the extreme uncleannefs of them. The *dragon*, we have feen, is an appellation, by which the devil is peculiarly diftinguifhed. The *beaft* and the *falfe prophet*, are fubordinate powers under his government; which the prefent fubject doth not require an explanation of. From their coming out of the mouth of the dragon, may be inferred, that they originated from him, as their principal: And their coming out of the mouths of the beaft, and falfe prophet, indicates their having previoufly entered them; and their being all intimately connected together.

* Revel. xvi. 13, 14.
† Luke iv. 33.

These spirits are all said to be spirits of devils, or *demons*, or *devilish spirits*, as the words may be translated—spirits of a diabolical nature. These, therefore, could not be the spirits of men likewise; nor could these *demons* be departed souls; as, I hope, such never originated from the dragon; nor possessed him; as he, together with the beast, and false prophet, must have been possessed by them, before they came out of their mouths. They were the several emissaries of these wicked powers, respectively sent by them to disturb the peace of the world.

Whence it appears, that they were under the command of the dragon; and were employed in his work; and therefore have all the characters of fallen angels. Even the *working of miracles* is ascribed to them; a power, I presume, above that of departed souls. But I leave the learned author, with whom I am concerned, to reconcile this positive proof of their power, in this respect, to his notion, that no miracles are wrought but by God alone.

From the whole of this passage, it appears, That possessing *demons* are so intimately connected with the devil; so much under his command; and that he is so much concerned ed in demoniacal poffeffions; that we may safely venture to affirm, that he is the chief author of them.

It is time now to take notice of some more direct arguments from scripture, which are used in the Effay, to fupport the doctrine of it: The chief of which occur in Sect. X. Prop. X. which contains this pofition.

"That the *doctrine* of demoniacal poffef-
"fions, inftead of being fupported by the
"Jewifh or Chriftian revelation, is utterly
"fubverted by both."

This is coming to the point: And if this pofition be made good; it muft be decifive againft poffeffions. In oppofition to it, I muft, in the firft place, obferve in general, that poffeffions are not properly matters of *doctrine*; but matters of *fact*: From which the doctrine concerning them refults of courfe. And if it be founded upon a fufficient number of facts, as I hope it appears to be, all that is faid in this chapter, or elfewhere, or indeed that can be faid againft it, will be of no avail to invalidate the truth of it.

This doctrine, as he calls it, is roundly difcarded in this chapter, out of the Old Teftament; together with all facts that can be be alledged in support of it. But how justly, will appear in the *appendix*; where of course it will fall under consideration.

What besides is of greatest regard in this chapter, is the interpretation, which is put upon a passage in one of St. *Paul's* epistles; which, if wrong; the rest of it will be looked upon, as of little account. The passage is this—*We know that an idol is nothing in the world**. On these words, it is observed, 1. " That by an idol, we are here to un-" derstand a heathen demon, or deity; and " not the mere image, or statue; which " represented him." For that would spoil the argument—And, 2. " That those idols, " or *demons*, here spoken of, were not de-" vils; but such human spirits, as the Gen-" tiles deified †." But be they either the one or the other, it is maintained, 3. That when it is said, *an idol is nothing in the world*, the meaning is, either, that this reputed deity hath no existence in nature; or that he hath no degree of that power, which his votaries ascribe to him; and is of no more account than if he did not exist ‡.

---

* 1 Cor. xii. 2. Essay, p. 122.
† Ib. p. 199.
‡ Essay on Demoniacks, p. 74.

And

And the non-existence, and *absolute nullity* of these deities, or *demons*, is the point, which is laboured to be proved, throughout the remaining part of this chapter.

Now if these premises are all right and true; the conclusion is certainly just, and indisputable, that, *demons* being mere nullities, there never could be a real demoniack, or possessed person; because there was no such thing in nature, for him to be possessed by.

But, on the other hand, if these *demons* are all deified human spirits; and if these are all annihilated; for they once had existence; what becomes of the doctrine of a future state? If those human spirits which happened to be deified by the heathens, were all reduced to nothing; we cannot say, that any other human souls, after they have left the body, have any existence, more than they; but must conclude, that they are all vanished into air, and a final period is put to their very Being.

The learned author of this argument, for it is all his own, I persuade myself, did not mean to carry it so far. Notwithstanding that, I do not see, how it can conclude less:
And

the Case of the Gospel Demoniacks. 193

And as he muſt grant, that it thus proves too much; we may ſafely venture to aſſert, that it proves nothing at all.

Great ſtreſs notwithſtanding is laid upon this interpretation of St. *Paul's* words. Let us therefore draw a little nearer to them; and ſee, what their real import is in themſelves; excluſively of any conſequences, which this ſenſe that is put upon them, is attended with.

At the very firſt view, one would be apt to think that the word *idol* ſignifies the material image. Our apoſtle determines it to this ſenſe, when, in addreſſing his *Corinthian* converts, he tells them; *Ye know that ye were Gentiles, carried away unto theſe* dumb *idols, even as ye were led* *. They very well knew, not only, that in their gentile ſtate, they were carried away unto theſe idols; but likewiſe, that theſe idols of wood and ſtone, before which they worſhiped, were *dumb*; and could not poſſibly have the faculty of ſpeech. But they could not know, that the gods themſelves, repreſented by them, were dumb and ſpeechleſs likewiſe. On the contrary, they were often ſuppoſed to ſpeak and converſe with men.

Our apoſtle himſelf furniſhes us with an inſtance of the ſentiments which their wor-

* 1 Cor. xii. 2. Gr. Ειδωλα αφωνα.

O ſhipers

shipers had of them, in this respect. *The gods are come down to us, in the likeness of men,* said the people of *Lystra*. And they called, *Barnabas*, *Jupiter*; and *Paul*, *Mercurius*; *because he was the chief speaker* *. The idols of the heathen, says the psalmist, *are silver, and gold, the work of men's hands. They have mouths, but they speak not: Eyes have they; but they see not. They have ears; but they hear not: Neither is there any breath in their mouths* †. This surely will be allowed to be the description of material idols; and not of the deities represented by them. The psalmist adds, *They that make them are like unto them: So is every one that trusteth in them.* Whence we are obliged to conclude, that if the idols have no existence, neither have their makers, nor those who confide in them. They are all non-entities alike.

What profiteth the graven image, saith the prophet, *that the maker thereof hath graven it? The molten image, and a teacher of lyes; that the maker of his work trusteth therein, to make dumb idols* ‡. *Woe unto him that saith unto the wood, awake; to the dumb stone, arise.* It

---

* Acts xiv. 12.

† Ps. cxxxv. 15.—cxv. 3. LXX. Ειδωλα.

‡ Ειδωλα κωφα, LXX. parallel to Ειδωλα αφωνα, of the Apostle.

shall teach. Behold, it is laid over with gold and silver; and there is no breath at all in the midst of it *. All this must surely be predicated of the graven and molten image.

The golden calf had sacrifice offered to him, as unto an idol †. Not unto the deity which it represented: Whether that were the *Egyptian Apis*; or the true god, as some think: Nor can it be pronounced of this golden calf, that it was absolutely nothing at all: Even then, when *Moses burnt it in the fire, and ground it to powder; strawed it upon the water, and made the children of Israel drink* ‡ *of it*. As fruitless will all attempts be, to make *St. Paul*'s idol in the place before us literally nothing.

St. Cyprian inveighs much against idols, in his treatise *De idolorum vanitate*: But he would have changed this title, and have written, *De idolorum nullitate;* had he been aware of our author's interpretation.

St. Chrysostom, on these words, *we know that an idol is nothing in the world*, very pertinently asks the following questions—*Do not idols exist? Have graven images no existence?* They do exist indeed: but they have no power. They are not gods, but stones

* Hab. ii. 18, 19. † Acts vii. 41. ‡ Exod. xxxii. 20.

and demons *. Understand these words, as you please; either of the stones, or the demons: For you see they take in both; and make your advantage of them. Both are included in the following passage of scripture, *They repented not of the works of their hands, that they should not worship devils, and idols of gold and silver, and brass, and stone, and of wood, which neither can see, nor hear, nor walk* †.

The explanation which the commentators give of this passage is,—that with regard to the matter of idols; it certainly is something, being made of gold, or silver, wood, or stone: But with regard to any virtue, or efficacy, or value, that can be in them; that they are things of nothing; of no use, or account; being representations of fictitious deities, which in truth are no gods; and equally impotent and insignificant, as the idols or images themselves ‡. But they all unanimously suppose, that by the idol

---

* Ουκ εςιν ουν ειδωλα; ουκ εςι ξοανα; εςι μεν, αλλ' ουκ εχει τινα ισχυν· Ουδε Θεοι εισιν, αλλα λιθοι, και δαιμονες. Hom. xx. in Cor. viii. 4.

† Rev. ix. 20.

‡ See Synopsis Crit. in loc.

is meaned, the material visible image, as the word imports *.

Enough hath been said, to expose the palpable absurdity of inferring the total nullity of idols from the text. This conceit cannot be maintained, but upon the principles of a late whimsical philosophy; that the visible world is all ideal, and imaginary; and that there is nothing *in rerum naturâ*, that hath any real existence.

This is the conclusion of the main argument, which is brought against the reality of demoniacal possessions; and we see how inconclusive it is, and how insufficient to support the inference that is drawn from it; " that there never was, nor can be, a real " demoniac †."

Akin to this, is the position we elsewhere meet with, in the following words, " We " have seen, that Christ, and his Apostles, " never assert the doctrine of possessions; but " on the contrary, entirely subvert it; when " they are professedly stating those doctrines,

---

* The word Ειδωλον is derived by the Lexicographers, from Ειδω, *video*; whence it properly signifies a visible image. And Ειδωλειον, 1 Cor. viii. 10. was the idol temple, wherein the idols, or images of the heathen gods were placed.

† Essay on Demoniacks, p. 240.

" which

" which they were immediately commission-
" ed and instructed to teach the world *."
Good God! Where is this to be seen? One
might expect to have found chapter and verse
quoted for so extraordinary an assertion. But
I can see no such thing in the essay; nor can I
conceive, to what part of it the reference is
made, unless it be to that place, which we
have been now considering; but which will
bear no such burden. Sure I am, there is no
such doctrine in scripture; it being so contrary
to many parts, and to the whole tenour of it.
Possessions, I observed, are not so properly
matters of doctrine, as matters of fact. The
fact, we have seen instances of in abundance:
And the doctrine arising from them is sufficiently evident of course; though it may
not be laid down in such a manner, and in
such places, as our author seems to dictate.

Instead of inferring from hence, " That
" Christ and his Apostles contradict them-
" selves, if by using the common language,
" with respect to demoniacks, they meant to
" countenance the opinion, on which it was
" grounded †:"—The right inference would
have been, from their using this language;
to infer, that they did most certainly mean
to countenance that opinion; and to establish
the truth of it.

* Essay on Demoniacks, p. 314.   † Ib.

It

It is not for nothing, that the change is every now and then put upon us; and that poffeffion is reprefented as matter of doctrine, inftead of fact. Doctrines are often doubtful, and liable to be controverted: But prove any thing to be a fact, and all doubt about it prefently vanifhes; nor is there any difputing againft real facts. Hence I conceived the likelieft method of deciding this controverfy, was to reduce it to a queftion of facts; and to produce inftances of it, as the beft proofs of the reality of the poffeffions, which were the fubject of it. The author of the effay agrees with me here concerning the weight of facts inftanced in; and reckons it as eafy to prove the reality of poffeffions in every inftance, as in any one. "If, fays he, you can prove the reality of "poffeffion in *one* inftance, from the lan- "guage of fcripture, you may prove it in "*all**." Many inftances of poffeffions have been here produced; and I flatter myfelf the reality of them hath been proved from both the fenfe and language of fcripture, in *all* and *every* one.

Let us proceed now to examine the fenfe of the primitive chriftians in this refpect.

* P. 131. no c.

The author of the essay says, "That the primitive Christians understood by *demons*, human spirits; and represents this, as the general opinion of the world." But how truly, will appear presently.

He quotes but one passage in support of it; out of one writer, *Justin M.* who mentions it only, as the opinion of the heathens; but not as his own; which proves to be very different from it; as may be collected from several parts of his works *.

In this very apology, from which the passage is taken, and on which so much stress is laid are these words—" The prince and ringleader of evil demons is called by us, the serpent, and satan, and the devil,"— as, says he, you may find in our books:

These books are none other than the books of holy Scripture, in which the devil and his angels are thus described. Are these human spirits?

It is a well known opinion of *Justins*, That *demons* were the offspring of angels,

* P. 4. This passage is as follows, Οἱ ψυχαις αποθανοντων λαμβανομενοι, και ῥιπτυμενοι ανθρωποι, ὡς δαιμονοληπτοι, και μαινομενους καλυσι παντες. Apol. i. p. 28. ed. *Thirlby*, see *Twells'* answer to *Sykes's* enquiry. p. 10. Ὁ αρχηγετης των κακων δαιμονων οφις καλειτοι, και σατανας, και διαβολος, κ. τ. λ. ib. 46.

by women, with whom they supposed them to cohabit *. And of the same opinion, however odd, were many of the Fathers: *Athenagoras, Clemens Alex. Tertullian, Lactantius*; and other primitive writers.

It is in allusion to this notion, I suppose, that the learned writer owns *Justin* seemed to believe in *demons*, of a different order from those that were of the human species; though he doth not choose to speak out. He owns farther, That *Justin* in his *Cohort. ad Græcos*, calls the devil, a *demon*; and speaks of the devil's deceiving our first parents. All this shews, That *Justin* is but a bad witness, that the primitive Christians believed possessing *demons* to have been human spirits; since we see he himself believed very differently of them, and their origin: And as our author cites him for calling the devil a *demon*; this is an authority point blank against himself; in the distinction he would fain make between *demons* and devils.

Justin likewise joins bad angels and *demons* together, and gives both the same epithets, as being of the same nature—men-

---

* Οἱ δ' ἄγγελοι παραβάντες τήνδε την τάξιν, γυναικῶν μίξεσιν ἡττήθησαν, και παῖδας ἐτέκνωσαν. Apol. ii. p. 46.

tions many men being δαιμονοληπ]ϗς, and ενεϱγεισθαι ὑπο των φαυλων δαιμονων, seized and possessed by these foul *demons*; whom the heathen sorcerers and magicians could not relieve them from; but who were healed; and continued to be healed, by many Christians; who overcame and chased away, τϛς κατεχοντας τϛς ανθρωπϛς δαιμονας, the *demons* which possessed them. He gives a large account of the horrid and shameful abuses, which poor mortals suffered from these infernal spirits, both in his first and second apology *.

Tertullian hath a whole chapter upon *demons*, their power and their operations. "Those malicious spirits," he says, "from "the beginning of man's creation, were "fatally auspicious in their first attempt "upon his ruin." Were these the deified souls of men? "And they continue to "inflict distempers upon their bodies; and "to throw them into sad disasters." And he joins *demons* with evil angels; which agitate men with furies, and extravagant uncleannesses †. *Clemens Alexandrinus* calls the devil, the prince of *demons* ‡. He is

---

* Apol. i. p. 10. Apol. ii. p. 112.
† Tert. Apolog. cap. xxii. ‡ Clem. Strom. lib. v.

styled

styled by *Cyril*, the *demon*, who is the author of evil, and the father of sin*. *Theodoret* calls him the man-slaying *demon*, and the father of lyes †, and makes mention of the devil, and of the *demons* that were under him. St. *Basil* says of the devil, that he was not created a devil; but that, having received the privileges of an angel, his nature was changed into that of a *demon*, and that he became a wicked *demon* ‡. *Origen* and his followers taught, that those wicked *demons* would again recover their pristine happy state in heaven; agreeably to his notions in other respects. And to mention no more, *Ignatius* calls the devil Δαιμονιον ασωματον, an unbodied, or rather bodiless *demon* §.

The learned writer acknowledges, that possessions were ascribed by many of the fathers, I believe he might say all, after the time of *Justin M.* to fallen angels; when, as he would have it, before his time, they were ascribed to human spirits. Though he brings no proof of it, but *Justin* himself, whom he presses into the service con-

---

* Cyril. Hom. p. vi. † Theodoret. in Divin. decret. cap. viii.   ‡ Basil. Hom. xxi.
§ Ignat. epist. ad Smyrnenses.

trary to his own perſuaſion, as we have ſeen. All the abovementioned fathers were *Juſtin's* contemporaries, and flouriſhed in the ſame age with him, or ſoon after. And one of them lived before him.

To find out the truth, in any caſe, we ſhould make uſe of all the helps that can be had; and to be ſatisfied concerning the notions of the primitive Chriſtians in this reſpect, we ſhould conſult as many of the primitive writers, as we can get any information from; and not pin ourſelves down to any one of them; were he ever ſo clear and conſiſtent, and were the proofs produced from him ever ſo unexceptionable. This would weigh but little againſt the unanimous ſuffrages of all the reſt.

But what would be ſtill more ſatisfactory, we ſhould go to the fountain-head; from which the primitive Chriſtians drew all their notions. They were taught early, that their moſt deadly enemy was the devil. And as ſuch, they were required expreſſly to renounce him, and his angels, at their very baptiſm *: And as a ſtill more ſolemn abrenunciation of him; the exorciſing of the devil was a moſt antient

* Conſtit. Apoſt. lib. vii. cap. 41.

initiating rite, which was used, in conjunction with the prayers of the church, for the deliverance of the *Neophyte*, or new christian, from the power of Satan *. And that it was thought effectual for this purpose, we have many testimonies from antient writers; being used, not as an incantation, or magical rite, as the heathen exorcisms were; but simply by praying, and invoking the name of *Jesus* over those that were possessed.

But we find nothing of exorcising, or renouncing departed human souls, nor any *demons*, who are supposed to have had no connection with the devil: And yet these were enemies more dreadful than the devil himself, if they were the authors of all the plagues and torments of the possessed.

The practice of the church in this respect furnishes the best proof of the sentiments of the primitive Christians, concerning the nature of those evil Beings, which were supposed to possess the bodies of men in those days; and is equal to a cloud of witnesses.

The fathers all agreed with the primitive church, as we have seen, in the per-

* Cave's Prim. Christ. part 1. cap. x.

suasion,

suasion, that possessing *demons* were none other, than the devil and his angels: And this was the opinion of Christians in general.

But as they were the vulgar among the heathens, who believed them to be the souls of men: So they were only the simpler sort of Christians who were led into that opinion. It may indeed seem strange to any thinking man, that any people, who had the use of their reason, should entertain an opinion so contrary to all the dictates of it. We have seen the absurdity of it*: And it is matter of some wonder whence it should arise. It may not therefore be amiss to attempt the accounting for it.

This is not a question of mere curiosity. The resolving of it will be of use in a religious view; and the case will appear to have been none other than this.

An opinion so monstrous could proceed only from the father of lies; and it may be fairly traced up to him. The wiser heathens were aware of his impositions in other respects: And the primitive fathers detected him in this particular. *Porphyry* owned, the devils deceived, not only

* P. 171.

the

the vulgar; but even the wifeft of the Greek philofophers, and poets *. And he fays, "There was a deceitful kind of them, "who turned themfelves into all fhapes; "and perfonated the gods, *demons*, and the "fouls of the deceafed †." The *demons* which they counterfeited muft have been good *demons*; and they perfonated the fouls of the dead in the bodies of the living.

The writer of the effay acknowledges, "That feveral philofophers taught, that the "heathen demons, as he calls them, were "evil fpirits of a rank fuperior to mankind, "and that thefe demons perfonated the fouls "of the dead, gods, and *genii*; and procured "themfelves to be worfhiped, under their "names ‡." And he quotes many heathen writers in fupport of that opinion.

As thefe demons perfonated the fouls of men, in other refpects: fo did they particularly in their entrance of men's bodies under the femblance of departed human fouls.

We are obliged to the learned writer for

* Porphyry apud Eufeb. præp. Evang. lib. iv. cap. 21, 22.

† Γενος απαταλης φυσεως, πανlαμορφον, και πολυτροπον, υποκρινομενον και Θεus, και δαιμονας, και ψυχας τεθνηκοlων. De abftinentiâ, lib. ii.

‡ Effay, p. 49.

some proofs of this kind; though he makes a quite different use of them.

St. Chrysostom informs us, that the possessing *demons* pretended they were the souls of certain deceased persons. " The demo-
" niacks cry out, says he, I am the soul of
" such a one. But this is no more than a
" false pretence, and a diabolical deception.
" For it is not the soul of the deceased, that
" so cries out; but the *demon* that feigns
" these things to deceive the hearers *."
And he elsewhere mentions it, as the particular practice of these *demons*, to say; " I
" am the soul of such a monk, in order that
" they might deceive the hearers †."

The learned writer farther acquaints us, with the testimony of a person; so late, as in the year 1564; who declared, " That
" he himself also" (as well, it seems, as some others) " had seen not a few demo-
" niacks, in whom the unclean spirits, when

---

* Οἱ δαιμονωντες βοωσιν, ὁτι ψυχη τȣ δεινος εγω. Αλλα και τȣτο σκηνη τις, και απατη διαβολικη. Ου γαρ ἡ ψυχη τȣ τετελευτεκοτος ες:ιν ἡ βοωσα· Αλλα ὁ δαιμων, ὁ ὑποκρινομενος ταυτα, ὡςε απατησαι τȣς ακȣοντες.

S. Chrysost. tom. ii. Conc. 28. in Matt. p. 196.

† Οἱ δαιμονες λεγȣσι, τȣ μοναχȣ τȣ δεινος ἡ ψυχη ειμι, φησι—απατωσι γαρ τȣς ακȣοντες.

Ib. Tom. v. Conc. 36. in Lazarum, p. 235.

" they

" they were adjured by a prieft, falfely faid, they were the fouls of certain perfons, who had been flain *."

This is turned into ridicule. The fact however is not contefted; and it is confonant with the above proofs from *St. Chryfoftom*, and what we elfewhere learn from him—That thefe wicked *demons*, when they gat poffeffion of men's bodies, perfonated the fouls of fome that were deceafed in them.—And the better to carry on the impofture, they inftilled into the minds of the fimple vulgar a no lefs pernicious opinion, that the fouls of the deceafed became *demons*; to infinuate the belief of their being nearly akin to each other; and to render their intercourfe the more familiar to men's minds, under whatever denomination.

They particularly infufed a belief into weak people, That the fouls of thofe that fuffered violent deaths, efpecially, were turned into *demons*. In this *Satan* had a double view: On the one hand, to difparage the

---

* Hieronymus magius, inquit, ego quoque dæmoniacos non paucos vidi; in quibus immundi fpiritus, dum a facerdote adjurentur, fe interfectorum quorundam animas effe mentirentur. Var. lect. lib. iv. cap. 12. Effay on Demoniacks, p. 51—53.

memory of the christian martyrs: And on the other, as he was a murderer from the beginning, to put it into the hearts of sorcerers and necromancers, to destroy the lives of many innocent children; upon a presumption, that their souls would become *demons*; and that then they would be subservient to them in their magical enchantments. Thus *Simon Magus* pretended to fetch up the souls of the prophets from the lower regions; and of children who had been slain, to assist him in magical arts *.

We are obliged to the same St. *Chrysostom* chiefly for these several informations, concerning the many pestilent opinions, which the grand adversary, and deceiver of mankind sowed among them, to ensnare their souls: Which the good father doth not fail to remonstrate against, in more places than one, of his works †.

I should

---

* Tert. de animâ, cap. lviii. Clem. recog. lib. ii. p. 513.

† Ολεθριον δογμα τοις πολλοις ενθειναι βυλομενοι, οιον, οτι αι ψυχαι των απελθοντων δαιμονες γινονται· ο μηδεποτε γενοιτο, μηδε μεχρις εννοιας λαβειν. S. Chrysost. Tom. ii. Conc. 28. in Matt. p. 196.

Ευταυθα πονηρον νοσημα της υμετερας εξελειν βυλομαι ψυχης. Και γαρ πολλοι των αφελεστερων νομιζυσι τας ψυχας

I should now have taken my leave of this father; but that I find it necessary to vindicate him from a misrepresentation of his own opinion. He is charged, "That at the very "time, that he is opposing the notion of the "souls of those who suffer a violent death, "becoming *demons*, he asserts, that the souls "of wicked men become such *."

His words, as faithfully as I can translate them, are, "Many of the simpler sort "think, that the souls of those who suffer "violent deaths become *demons*. But it is "not so. It is not. For they are not the "souls of those that *die* by violence, who "become *demons*; but the souls of those that "*live* in their sins: Their nature," as he immediately adds, "not being changed; "but their choice being to imitate the wick- "edness of those evil spirits †." And to this he subjoins several very pertinent passa-

ψυχας των βιαιω θανατω τελευτωντων δαιμονας γινεσθαι. Ουκ ιςι δε τυτο· ουκ ιςιν. Ib. tom. v. com. 36. in Lazarum, p. 235.

* Essay on Demoniacks, p. 52, note.

† Ου γαρ αι ψυχαι των βιαθανατωντων δαιμονες γινονται. Αλλα αι ψυχαι των εν αμαρτημασι ζωντων. Ου της ουσιας αυτων μεταβαλλομενης, αλλα της προαιρεσεως (αυτων) την εκεινων μιμυμενης κακιαν. Chrysost. 16.

ges of scripture, with very proper distinctions and remarks; to justify the accounting of those, who *live* in their sins, to resemble *demons* too much in their devilish tempers and lives, though there be no change in their natures. To say that the souls of those who live in sin, become devils, might be understood as an easy figure of speech, without these explanations.

It was not possible for any writer to explain, and guard his meaning better. But there is no guarding against the mutilating of an author's expressions: Whereby he may be made to say any thing; be it ever so different from the real meaning.

I have dwelt longer upon this subject, than I intended. But it may not be without its use; by such instances to awake supine mortals; and excite their vigilance against that subtil enemy of their salvation, who is ever watchful of his prey, and daily lying in wait to deceive. He hath various arts and stratagems to circumvent unwary souls; and his resources are never exhausted.

Being, by the light of the gospel, detected; and restrained from his more open, and grosser attempts; and from any known, and palpable possessions of men's bodies; he goes
now

now a more secret and covert way to work: For he still *worketh*, though invisibly, *in the children of disobedience.*

As we see no instances of possessions, God be praised, in these times, which we can with certainty pronounce to be such: And as there have been many impostures of this kind; the deceitful adversary would fain persuade us, there are not, nor ever were, any real possessions at all; and employs his emissaries to argue, and banter us out of the belief of them; than which nothing can give him greater advantage against us; as thereby he may come upon us by surprize, and lead us captive at his will. Many, I doubt not, there are, who entertain this opinion, and defend it, from an honest, and good heart. I would nevertheless earnestly intreat all such to consider, whether they may not undesignedly be doing his work; and, while they think they are rendering God service, whether they may not be co-operating with the common enemy, to their own, and their fellow-creatures destruction.—Whether he may not be at their elbow; and they haply be found to fight against God?

However the antients differed about the nature of *demons*; there was no difference between them about their exiftence. The heathens in general; their philofophers, as well as the vulgar; the antient Jews, and the primitive Chriftians, agreed in the reality of their Being; and of their poffeffions. Nor was there any doubt among them in this refpect; unlefs it was among fuch as were of atheiftical or libertine principles, who denied the immortality of the foul. Of this fort were the *Epicureans* among the heathens, and the *Sadducees* among the *Jews*: Who are brought to patronize the opinion of their non-exiftence. *Lucian**, and *Celfus*, are among the worthies that fupport it; and *Rouffeau* is placed at the head of them.

To thefe might have been added, *Pomponatius, Vaninus, Hobbes, Spinofa,* and *Bekker*; who, it hath been obferved, have patronized the opinion, that poffeffions were nothing more than natural difeafes †: And who are

---

* *Lucian* wrote his *Philo-pfeudes* againft the exiftence of feparate fpirits. He fays of *Democritus* of *Abdera*—Οὕτω βεβαίως ἐπίςευσε μηδὲν εἶναι τὰς ψυχὰς ἔτι ἔξω γενομένας τῶν σωμάτων.

† See the ufual interpretation of Δαίμονες and Δαιμονία, in N. T. afferted in a fermon, by Dr. Hutchinfon. p. 30.

all well known to have been profane and atheistical writers.

Mr. *Mede* is placed at the head of those that are of this opinion among our modern divines, and his authority is truly respectable. But those that press it into the service of their cause, would not have so much reason for triumphing in it, if his sense were taken altogether. It may be seen in one view; and is well vindicated in a late learned dissertation on demoniacks*.

As for the opinions of physicians, antient or modern, I think they do not carry much weight; as it is well known, they are too apt to resolve every kind of *phænomena* into natural causes.

St. *Luke's* authority is sufficient to over-rule them all: And they would all have submitted to it, if they had paid him but his due regard, and that which they fail not to shew to other antients, who have gone before them in the profession.

Had Dr. *Mead*, particularly, weighed with impartiality, *the force and meaning of the evangelist's words*; which he acknowledges, that, as a physician, the divine writer well understood

* Dissert. on Demoniacks, p. 32.

underſtood; he would not have deviated from the ſenſe of them, ſo much as he did; nor be biaſſed by any ties of kindred into the contrary opinion.

The qualifications of the *beloved phyſician* as a witneſs, have already been taken notice of*. That his evidence, and that of the other evangeliſts, which hath ſtood unimpeached above ſeventeen centuries, ſhould now be thus diſputed, and perverted from its natural meaning, is contrary to all the laws of evidence; hath a tendency to deſtroy the faith of all hiſtory, and to introduce an univerſal ſcepticiſm.

The credit of the holy evangeliſts is to be held ſacred and inviolable, for the ſake of the great truths which they deliver; and which, if impaired in ſome reſpects, will be expoſed to the like treatment in others. None of theſe truths are of greater importance, than thoſe, on which the whole depends; the miracles which were wrought, in atteſtation of it. To weaken the force of any of theſe miracles; and interpret them away, is ſhaking the foundation of our holy religion. The miracles of healing the ſick,

* P. 120.

and casting out devils, are in their nature distinct; and that distinction is always preserved in the narration. The casting out of devils was a more signal kind of miracles, and these were greater miracles likewise, than the healing of any diseases; as bodily diseases in general cannot be supposed so difficult of cure; as to overcome, and dislodge these personal and most inveterate enemies of mankind; and to cure those distempers too, which were inflicted by them. For as mere natural diseases proceed from natural causes; these causes are often removed, and the diseases remedied, by skilful physicians, in a natural way, by the use of proper means. The difference in the cure of such diseases, by the divine physician, lay in his healing them, without the use of means, instantaneously, by a word's speaking. And this was truly miraculous. But if comparison may be made, of one miracle to another: And, I think, such comparison is in this case justifiable; nay necessary, when these miracles are so much disparaged.— This being the case, it surely must be allowed to have been a greater miracle to heal the disease; and to disarm, and *bind the strong man* likewise that caused it; and to turn him

him out of his unlawful poſſeſſion. Here therefore was a double miracle. The ſeventy diſciples ſingled out theſe miracles; as the greateſt they had ever been impowered to perform. *Lord, even the devils are ſubject to us, through thy name:* Thus triumphing, as it were, over all the power of the enemy. The author of the eſſay on demoniacks cannot help acknowledging the high rank and weight, which theſe miracles bear in the ſcale and eſtimation of miracles. "Theſe "miracles," ſays he, "of thoſe performed "upon the goſpel demoniacks, are always "ſpoken of in the *New Teſtament*, with "ſingular emphaſis and diſtinction. Scarce "are any other miracles more frequently "and circumſtantially deſcribed." He might have ſaid, that ſcarce any are *ſo* frequently, and circumſtantially deſcribed. "It required an extraordinary degree of "faith to undertake them;" as for inſtance in the caſe of the lunatick, mentioned, Matt. xvii. 20. Mark ix. 29. Theſe he accounts "difficult miracles." "The ſeventy, he "ſays, as juſt now obſerved, were filled "with exultation and triumph, when they "found themſelves enabled to cure demoni-"acks." The ſpectators were filled with religious

religious aftonifhment, and awe at thefe wonderful miracles *.

Very handfomely faid indeed! One would think no lefs, than that he was, in good earneft, difplaying the fuperior excellency of thefe miracles. Who would ever imagine, that all this was no more than a prelude to his finking them to the level of fuch miracles, as were performed for the healing of the fick only?

But what is yet much more reprehenfible, is, that fuch a collection of the low, indecent, juggling tricks of profane exorcifts and magicians, fhould be tacked to the above fair defcription of our Saviour's miracles on the demoniacks; without any *falvo* to prevent their being paralleled with each other; and that the idea of thefe filly and ridiculous charms fhould be left, in a manner, laft upon the minds of the readers, at the conclufion of this performance. This is fuch management, as muft raife the indignation of every ferious chriftian; as well as his zeal to refcue them from fuch unworthy treatment.

To this purpofe, it fhould be obferved, that the merit of thefe miracles hath not yet been done juftice to; and that they have ftill

* See Effay on Demoniacks, p. 408.

farther excellences. For thefe were miracles performed upon the fouls, as well as bodies of men; and as the foul is much more precious, and of greater concern, than the body; fo thefe miracles were more merciful, and beneficial, in proportion.

The healing of bodily difeafes was undoubtedly a very great benefit to mankind: But the healing of the diftempers of their fouls was furely a greater benefit ftill; and the greateft mercy that could be vouchfafed to poor mortals, who grievoufly laboured under them.

Our Saviour, when he cured the Demoniack, not only ejected the evil fpirit; but at the fame time, no lefs wonderfully fubdued the diabolical temper, which inftigated the wretched fufferer to fuch acts of rage and cruelty, againft himfelf, and all about him:—affaulting and wounding all who came near him—fpreading terror all around him—tearing his own flefh—cutting himfelf with ftones—and attempting to deftroy hmifelf.—For fuch a one to be made calm and compofed in an inftant; and to be reftored to his right mind; was fuch a miracle of mercy, as would leave the moft lafting impreffions.

Ac-

Accordingly, it may reasonably be presumed, that most, if not all the demoniacks, who had been cured by our Lord, and his disciples, were so deeply affected by, and so thoroughly convinced of, the divine power that displayed itself, in their deliverance; as to become sincere converts, and true disciples to our Saviour.

Of this we have one remarkable instance in fact, of the man, who had the legion of devils cast out of him, being found sitting at the feet of *Jesus*, listning to his doctrine, and as may well be supposed, being in his right mind; and beseeching him, that he might be with him; and admitted as one of his disciples. And though *Jesus* judged he would be of more service to the cause of his religion, by continuing in his own country; to convince an unbelieving people, of the greatness of God's mercy towards him; the readiness of his obedience, as well as the sincerity of his conversion, appears, from his going immediately, and publishing throughout the whole city, and all the region of *Decapolis, how great things Jesus had done unto him.* And as this was the case in one instance, it may be presumed, it was the same in many others.

Now,

Now the representing of this whole set of great, astonishing, and most beneficial miracles, as being no more than curing bodily diseases; the putting of both these kinds of miracles on the same footing; the resolving of the one, into the other; and confounding both together; is surely very injurious to the former; is sinking their value, and depreciating of them to a great degree; and causing them to be, in a manner, lost, among these latter; and, I may venture to say, lesser miracles. It is weakening the evidence of christianity in general; and depriving it of a considerable number of the great miracles, on which it is built.

An argument sufficient for this purpose ought to amount to nothing less than demonstration. A question of such importance, that affects christianity in so essential a part, ought to be debated with great caution and candour; and requires the soundest, and most uncontrovertible principles to be decided upon. But an hypothesis, that is built upon no good principle at all, nor any solid foundation whatsoever—that rests upon the fanciful, the vain, and the uncertain opinions of men — that militates

against

against the tenour, as well as letter of scripture; and against the whole analogy of faith—that opposes the sentiments of the most respectable of the antients of all denominations; both after christianity, and since; till within these latter times—that is countenanced by very few modern divines of character, or soundness of faith—And is patronized chiefly by such, among antients and moderns, as are a disgrace to any cause—Such an hypothesis, I trust, will not be capable of convincing any serious enquirer; who was not, beforehand, under some prejudices in its favour; though it may be likely enough to meet with reception, and countenance, among lukewarm, and half christians; and such as are disposed to sink christianity to an ebb, which is but a few degrees above deism; the manifest design of these, and such like productions being, to bring down christianity to the level of natural religion; which every one will have the modeling of, by the square of his own reason; whereby he will frame it to his liking; and make as pliable, and good-natured a religion of it, as he pleases. And by that means, at length, men will come to be without any thing,

thing, that can deferve the name of religion; and will live fo, as without God in the world.

Let us hold faft the profeffion of our faith, without wavering, and earneftly contend for it, as it was once delivered to the faints; that we may ftand perfect, and complete, in all the will of God.

AN APPENDIX;

CONSISTING OF

An ESSAY

ON

SCRIPTURE DEMONOLOGY.

To complete this enquiry—To have a fuller, and more comprehensive view of the subject of it—to have juster and more adequate notions of those invisible Beings, about which it is conversant—And to form the better judgment of this controversy; so as that every one may determine concerning it for himself, with the greater precision, and accuracy; it will be necessary to have recourse to the word of God; in which alone we can hope to have such certain information, as can fully be confided in;

or any well-grounded satisfaction in this respect.

To this end, it will be requisite to bring together into one view, though not all, yet the chief and principal accounts, hints, and allusions, which lie dispersed in the scriptures, that can contribute to cast light on a subject, which hath not been professedly treated on before, by any one within my knowledge, or recollection*; in order to attempt something of a system of Scripture-demonology; the imperfection of which it is hoped will be excused, as it is but a kind of first essay.

For it is not to be expected, that any direct records or formal proofs, should be produced, especially out of the Old Testament, of every thing relating to this subject. It will, I hope, be thought sufficient, if the main doctrine be clearly established; while concomitant circumstances, and incidental matters, relating to it, are made out to a tolerable degree of probability, at least; by fair inference, and analogy to the whole.

How much something of this kind is wanted appears too plainly, from the treatise

* K. *James* I. wrote a treatise on demonology at large, which doth not answer the intent of this undertaking.

taken

taken notice of in the foregoing enquiry, as well as from several other writings of the same tendency; whence the *Sadducean* creed; that *there is neither angel, nor spirit*, seems to be reviving, and getting ground apace among us.

God, in his holy word, hath been pleased to warn us of the existence of a certain wicked spirit, branded by the denomination of the *Devil*; who is therein set forth to be a most inveterate enemy to him, and all mankind.

This Being, we learn, in his first estate, when he came out of the hands of his Creator, was an angel of light, holy in his nature, like the other holy angels of God. This may be inferred from his name *Lucifer*; which in itself is a title of honour; and alludes to his having been an angel of light, in his original state. For it signifies, *The Harbinger of light*, as its correspondent Hebrew name, הילל, imports; that is, *The resplendent*. Accordingly, he is in the context called, *Son of the morning* *.

This once glorious Being proved rebellious against his Sovereign Lord and Maker, and revolted from his government: Whereupon

---

* Isa. xiv. 12.

he was degraded from the high rank, in which he had been stationed in the angelick choir; and was cast down out of heaven. The Son of God was witness to his downfall. In allusion to which he saith, *I saw Satan, as lightning, fall from heaven* *. A noble comparison, which conveys a very striking idea of that glorious nature, and that exalted state, from which he had been precipitated.

The prophet likewise, though his thoughts were occupied about other matters, alludes to this catastrophe. *How art thou fallen from heaven, O Lucifer, Son of the morning? Thou hast said in thine heart, I will ascend into heaven: I will exalt my throne above the stars of God—I will ascend above the heights of the clouds: I will be like the most High* †. Whence the motives of his apostacy seem to have been pride and ambition. Accordingly he is every where in scripture described, as the arch-rebel against his creator; and the great opposer of his will in the government of the world.

Being fallen from heaven, he was cast down to the earth; where he gave early

* Luke x. 18. † Isa. xiv. 12, 13, 14.

proofs of his malignancy. For finding himself unable to contend with his Maker directly; he betook himself to oppose him indirectly in his image man.

For no sooner had God made man, and placed him, with his consort, in a state of happiness; than the devil projected to disturb his moral government of the world; and as far as lay in his power, to ruin and destroy this innocent pair. With this view, he entered the body of a serpent; which was the fittest instrument for his purpose; and *by his subtilty, beguiled Eve* *.

That the devil actually did take possession of the body of a serpent, and spake out of it, when he tempted the woman, is a truth founded on scripture, and appears from many passages of it. Hence, particularly he is called by the name of the *great Dragon*, and the *old serpent*; alluding to this primitive one. This possession is analogous to other subsequent possessions of his; and more especially to that of swine; which serve to illustrate and confirm each other. And as an ass hath been made to speak articulately, why might not the serpent's organs be fitted for the purpose, as well? If indeed it was through his mouth that the

* 2 Cor. xi. 3.

devil spake; and not out of his belly ; as ventriloquists are said to have done.

This likewise is agreeable to the notions of the heathens concerning evil spirits ; who reckoned them to have so much versatility in their impositions upon mankind, that they could turn themselves into all shapes ; and assume the bodies of all sorts of animals, which they found fittest for carrying on their deceitful designs *.

The literal sense of this account of *Eve's* temptation having been questioned, and controverted, not many years ago; and an attempt having been made to interpret it allegorically ; this intent hath been fully frustrated ; and the historical and literal meaning clearly vindicated, and established †.

The direful consequences of the fall of man, brought about by the practices of the Tempter, the reality of which is too well ascertained by the effects; and our

---

* Γενος απαταλης φυσεως, παντομορφον, και πολυτροπον. Porph. lib. ii. de abstinentiâ.

Περι ζωοις ομοιεμενοι προσιασι τες ανθρωπες.   Porph. apud Eufeb. præcep. evang. lib. iv. cap. 23.

† See particularly the historical sense of the Mosaick account of the Fall proved and vindicated.

deliverance

deliverance from it, by the mercies of our Redeemer, would carry us into too wide a field to expatiate upon; and too diftant from this defign.

The devil inceffantly purfued his malicious intentions againft the human race; when, there being no more than two fons born to *Adam*, he inftigated one of them to murder the other. For this, we find in fcripture, is to be imputed to him; which informs us, That *Cain was of that wicked one, and flew his brother* *—That *the devil was a murderer from the beginning; and abode not in the truth; becaufe there is no truth in him. When he fpeaketh a lye,* that he *fpeaketh of his own; for he is a lyar, and the father of it* †. He is likewife called, *The wicked one; The enemy; The adverfary* of men; *The tempter;* all by way of eminence; which denotes him to be fuperlatively fuch; and to have all thofe malignant qualities in the higheft degree.

Befides thefe appellations, he is called *Satan, Beelzebub; Belial, Abaddon, Apolluon,* that is, *The deftroyer; The prince of the power of the air, The prince,* and *god of this world.*

* Jo. iii. 12. † Jo. viii. 44.

With regard to his office and employment, his power, and sway in the world; he is said *to deceive the whole world*—To be *the accuser of his brethren, and to accuse them before God night and day* *. He is said to be *going to and fro in the earth* †; *and to be walking up and down in it, as a roaring lion, seeking whom he may devour* ‡. He is said to have the power of death; and is called, *The spirit that now worketh in the children of disobedience — working with all power, and signs, and lying wonders; and with all deceiveableness of unrighteousness, in them that perish*. He is said to busy himself in sowing tares among the wheat—*to blind the minds of them that believe not*; *lest the light of the glorious gospel of Christ should shine unto them*.

We are farther told, That when some hear the word, *Satan cometh immediately, and taketh away the word out of their hearts; lest they should believe, and be saved*—That this *Satan is sometimes transformed into an angel of light*; such as he once was before—

---

* Rev. xii. 9, 10. † Job i. 7.
‡ 1 Pet. v. 8. Heb. ii. 14. Eph. ii. 2. 2 Thes. ii. 9, 10. 2 Cor. iv. 4. Mark iv. 15. Luke viii. 12. 2 Cor. xi. 14. Luke xvii, 31.

That

That he hath a defire to have us, that he may fift us, as wheat—That he is ever watching to get advantage of us; and to *hinder us in running the race that is set before us**—And that many fall into his fnares; from which, if they do not recover themfelves, they are taken captives by him at his will. Laftly, our adverfary, the Devil, is faid, upon occafion, to come down unto us, having great wrath: And that he had the hardinefs to difpute with *Michael* the Arch-angel, about the body of *Mofes*; and to wage war in heaven.

From this view, it appears, that this Being is malignant in an extraordinary degree—That, as God is the author of all good; fo the Devil is the author of all evil—That he is the evil principle; as evil is inherent in him, and originates from him—That he introduced it into the world; and ftill continues to inftigate, and excite mankind to it—That he commits evil, without ceafing; and practifes all forts, and degrees of it—That he not only was the firft finner; but that he ftill finneth; and hath continued to fin from the beginning: And

* 1 Thef. ii. 18. 2. Tim. ii. 26. Revel. xii. 7, 12.

that he who committeth sin is of the Devil; who is the father of all such—That he is at the bottom of most, if not all the gross sins and wickednesses, that are committed in the world; as for instance, of all the murders, massacres, persecutions, wars, and destructions of mankind—Of all idolatry, and false worship; and falshood of all kind—all gross errors, and all corruptions, and deviations from truth, which affect religion and morality; all impiety, irreligion, prophaneness; and all vile affections, and unnatural lusts proceed from him, or are secretly fomented by him.

In a word, it is manifest, that his hatred and malice; his subtilty, his vigilance, his revengefulness, is such, that he is the most dangerous, the most inveterate, and implacable enemy of mankind: And that we should never be able to withstand his power to hurt and destroy us, both in body and soul, if he were permitted to exert it to the utmost.

But thanks be to God, and our gracious Redeemer, the power of the evil one is not unlimited. The Lord God omnipotent reigneth over all; and is mighty to help, and deliver us from the jaws of the destroyer.

The

The Lord of hosts is with us; the God of Jacob is our refuge*.

If we do not give place to the Devil—If we manfully resist him, and are steadfast in the faith, he will flee from us †.

The captain of our salvation hath furnished us with a complete suit of christian armour, in the use of which he will enable us to be *more than conquerors, through him who strengtheneth us.* And if we will be advised by the Apostle, *to put on the breast-plate of righteousness—to take the helmet of salvation, and the sword of the spirit, which is the word of God; together with prayer, and watching thereunto with all perseverance, and above all, taking the shield of faith*—having thus *put on the whole armour of God*, we shall *be strong in the Lord, and in the power of his might*; and shall *be able to stand, in the evil day, against the wiles of the Devil; and to quench all the fiery darts of the wicked one* ‡.

The Devil was not alone in the transgression. He found means to seduce a numerous company of the other angels of God; and to draw them into the apostacy with him; whence they were all involved in the

* Pf. xlvi. 7, 11.
† Eph. iv. 27. 1 Pet. v. 9. James iv. 7.
‡ Eph. iv. 10. 18.

same fate. Thus we learn, that, having failed in their duty, and sinned; they consequently kept not their first estate: Or, they kept not their principality; for so the word Αρχη is often translated in the New Testament; and thus it is rendered in the margin here.—Having failed in keeping the principality, which they were invested with in their first estate; and having thereupon quitted their posts and stations in heaven; and *left their own* proper *habitation* there, *God spared them not; but cast them down into Hell; and delivered them into chains of darkness, to be reserved unto judgment* *. Or, as St. *Jude* expresses it, in the parallel place, with very little difference—*He hath reserved them in everlasting chains, under darkness, unto the judgment of the great day* †.

We are elsewhere told, That *there was war in Heaven. Michael and his angels fought against the dragon: And the dragon fought, and his angels; and prevailed not; neither was their place found any more in Heaven. And the dragon, called the Devil, and Satan—was cast out into the earth; and his angels were cast out with him* ‡.

* 2 Pet. ii. 4.   † Jude 6.
‡ Rev. xii. 7, 8, 9.

But now here seems to be some inconsistency. St. *Peter* and St. *Jude* say, that the fallen angels were cast into *Hell*; and reserved there in everlasting chains of darkness. St. *John* says, 'The Devil was cast out into the *earth*; and his angels were cast out with him; into the earth likewise, it may be presumed: And he elsewhere says, he was bound, and cast into the bottomless pit; and shut up there; but for a thousand years; and afterwards loosed for a little season.*

And we have seen from numberless places of scripture, cited in the foregoing enquiry, that the Devil, and his angels, have had the liberty of roaming about in the earth, and doing much mischief in it.

Now to reconcile these different accounts is the difficulty: And I wonder it was not laid hold on in the essay on demoniacks; as an objection of greater weight might be drawn from it, than any I see there.

To remove this difficulty, it should be considered, that we know nothing of the world of spirits, but what God hath vouchsafed to reveal to us. His government of it is a perfect mystery; and far above out of

* Ch. xx. 3.

our sight. There are many mysteries in the constitution and government of this visible world—many dispensations and truths incomprehensible to us; and many different measures planned, and pursued, which seem inconsistent with, and irreconcileable to each other; which yet are the result of consummate wisdom, and perfectly reconcileable in themselves.

Mr. *Mede* was aware of the seeming contradiction; and to remove it, renders those passages of St. *Peter* and St. *Jude, reserved,* not *in,* but *unto* chains of darkness; implying, that they were not to be doomed to their eternal prisons, till the day of final judgment. To which sense, he thinks, the Devil's expostulation with our Saviour refers, *Art thou come hither to torment us before the time?* Alluding to this time of the judgment of the great day. And he brings the opinion of several of the fathers, which seem to give some countenance to him; as they thought, that the fallen angels had their present abode in the air, or atmosphere of this earth; and that this region was their intermediate prison. His sense, in his own words, is, " That the evil spirits which sinned, being adjudged to hellish torments,
were

were caſt out of Heaven, into this lower region; there to be reſerved, as in a priſon, for chains of darkneſs, at the day of judgment *."

But I think there is another way of reconciling thoſe two texts, with the many others, which expreſsly inform us, that the Devil and other evil ſpirits ply at large on this earth, and buſy themſelves among the inhabitants of it: The method I would propoſe for reconciling theſe differences, is ſubmitted to the reader, and is as follows:

That the Devil, and his angels, when they left their heavenly manſions, were, one and all, immediately baniſhed to Hell; and there condemned to continue in a ſtate of impriſonment, until the judgment of the great day:—But that God, in the mean time, for wiſe ends, in his moral government of this world, thought fit to permit ſome of them to be occaſionally releaſed out of their infernal priſons; in order to make uſe of them, as the executioners of his wrath, and of his judgments, upon a ſinful world; and likewiſe for correction and mercy in the end—That they are appointed by him to be

* Mr. Mede's works, vol. I. diſ. iv. p. 30. And Whitby on 2 Pet. ii. 4.

the licensed scourges of wicked men; and are made use of likewise for the trial of the faith and obedience of mankind in general, by the various temptations, which God permits them to be exercised with by them; and for many other wise purposes of his providence.

When they are employed in this manner, I apprehend they are at the same time kept under severe discipline; and have laws, and regulations assigned them, which they are tied down to a strict observance of—That they are not enlarged out of their confinement, but in certain numbers; for limited times; and for special purposes.—That they have their several commissions; and are kept under restraint, and controul, in the execution of them.—And in this state, are like prisoners at large, dragging their chains after them—That in some ages, they are released, and let out in greater numbers; and suffered to infest some persons, and some parts of the world, more than others; in proportion to the wickedness of them that dwell therein.

We have some hints in scripture, which seem to favour conjectures of this kind. *Art thou come hither to torment us before the time?*

I.

time? Possibly a certain limited time, which had been assigned for this party of wicked spirits, to return to their infernal mansions. They besought him, that he would not command them to go into the deep, εις τον αβυσσον; *the bottomless pit*, as we generally translate: The same probably with ταρταρος, whence comes ταρταρωσας; which is translated, *cast down into Hell**. They begged a reprieve for some time longer, that they might continue in the country, or even be permitted to enter the bodies of swine; rather than, as yet, to be remanded to that place of perpetual and most exquisite torments.

The Devil himself, who had been suffered to go about before as a roaring lion, was, at a certain period, bound for a thousand years, by an angel, which came down from Heaven; having the key of the bottomless pit, and a great chain in his hand: And he cast him into the bottomless pit; and shut him up; and set a seal upon him—till the thousand years should be fulfilled: And after that he must be loosed for a little season †. From these places, and some others, and especially from this last, it

---

* 2 Pet. ii. 4.   † Revel. xx. 1, 2, 3.

seems to appear, That the Devil, and his angels, though imprisoned in Hell, yet are not all so closely confined there; but that they are occasionally enlarged for limited times, to execute the will of the Almighty in the earth.

The description of the bottomless pit—it being committed to the custody of a certain angel—his seizing of his prisoner, the Devil; who it seems was at large before—His binding, and shutting of him up, for a certain period, and releasing him again—The key—The great chain—The seal, all indicate the greatest certainty, strictness, and punctuality, in orders relating to it, and its wretched inhabitants; and likewise in the execution of them.

If this conjecture be admitted, the texts relating to the confinement of the Devil, and his angels, on the one hand, and to their enlargement on the other, labour under no inconsistency; but are in perfect agreement with each other.

To proceed, as it was just now observed, that the Devil and his angels are subject to the divine controul and government: So it may be inferred, from several passages of scripture, that they have some sort of government among themselves.

They

They muſt originally have been united under one head, with proper leaders over them, in the conſpiracy which they formed, and in the war, which they waged in heaven. Accordingly we find, that the Devil and his angels are formed into a kind of confederacy, and conſtitute ſome ſort of government, over which he preſides as chief; with ſubordinate principalities, and powers, and rulers of darkneſs, under him—That *Satan* hath a kingdom; that it is united in itſelf; and the conſequence of a diviſion in it, is implied in theſe words of our Saviour, *If Satan be divided againſt himſelf, how can his kingdom ſtand?* He is *the prince of the devils*; and *the prince of the power of the air*; and every ſovereign prince muſt have ſubjects to reign, and bear rule, over; and to live and act in obedience to his commands. There are ſeveral ranks of evil ſpirits, with chieftains over them. The apoſtle firſt mentions *principalities and powers*, in general. Then he informs us of rulers *of darkneſs in this world*; by which are underſtood terreſtrial evil ſpirits; who have their abode upon earth; and after that, he takes notice of *ſpirits of wickedneſs*, or wicked ſpirits, *in high places*: Which are ſuppoſed to be ſuch as occupy the regions of the air: And he intimates,

intimates, that we have both the terrestrial, and the aerial ones, to wrestle, and contend with.

All these considerations shew how formidable our spiritual enemies are; and how necessary it is, that we should *be strong in the Lord, and in the power of his might*; and *put on the whole armour of God, that we may be able to stand against the wiles of the Devil**. Our comfort is, That *the captain of our salvation* hath not only furnished us, as observed above, with a complete suit of christian armour, to enable us to withstand them; but that he hath likewise spoiled these *principalities and powers*; and divested them in a good measure, of their great strength; and *openly triumphed over them in his cross* †.

We do not find in the short history of the bible any express mention of Devils, or other evil spirits; or of any that dealt with them, in the first age of the world. In the patriarchal age, we read of good angels often visiting and conversing with holy men; revealing God's will to them; and rescuing them from dangers; and among others, not unlikely, from the incursions of evil spirits;

* Eph. vi. 10, 11, 12.   † Col. ii. 15.

as they seem to have taken such men under their special care and protection. But of evil spirits we indeed find no express mention in that period.

Though false worship and idolatry, of which they were both the authors, and the objects, had appeared, and grown to a great head, in some countries; even before the patriarchal age. For *Abraham*, and his family had been cast out, and fled from *Ur* of the *Chaldees*, because they would not follow the gods of their fathers, and worshiped the God of Heaven *.

And even this family itself, in which the worship of the true God had been set up, and preserved, was not entirely free from all tincture of superstition and idolatry; of which *Laban's Teraphim* are a proof †. Nor will I maintain, there was no charm, or fascination meant, in *Jacob's pilled rods*, and in his laying them before the stronger ewes, that they might conceive *ring-streaked, speckled*, and *spotted lambs* among them ‡. For with what other intent was this contrivance made use of? Even *Joseph* had his divining cup §.

* Gen. xi. 31. Judith v. 7, 8. † Gen. xxxi. 30.
‡ Ch. xxx. 37. § Ch. xliv. 5.

This brings us down to the history of the children of *Israel* in *Egypt*. We here read of magicians, sorcerers, magical arts and inchantments exercised by them on several occasions. All idolatrous nations were much addicted to such professions and practices; and Egypt was, among all antient nations, the most immersed in idolatry, and magick likewise. Recourse was often had by them to sorcerers and magicians, in all difficult cases, and arduous concerns; about which they proposed to consult their gods; and particularly for obtaining from them an insight into futurity, which mankind was ever addicted to pry into: And the gods, whom they consulted, the scripture informs us, were devils, and not gods*.

The first occasion on which we find magicians were consulted in *Egypt* was for the interpretation of *Pharaoh's* dream: Whose *spirit being troubled, he sent, and called for all the magicians of Egypt, and all the wise men thereof* †. But all their wisdom now failed them. None of them could interpret the monarch's dream. And the interpretation of it was reserved by God for *Joseph*. However in about three generations after this time,

* Deut. xxxii. 17. 1 Cor. x. 20.
† Gen.

time, the magicians and wife men of *Egypt* made such amazing proficiency in the knowledge of their dark arts; or at least were so successful in the practice of them, as not to be paralleled by any who dealt in them, in any other age, or nation, either before, or after.

In the time of *Moses*, *Pharaoh* appears to have had much confidence in his magicians. For when *Moses* applied to him for the release of the *Israelites*, he seems to have put the proof of his mission upon miracles; and to have been ready to rival him in them. This, I think, is clearly implied in the text, *shew a miracle for you* *: And that in consequence of such a challenge it was, that *Aaron* turned his rod into a serpent. Upon which *Pharaoh* presently *called the wise men, and sorcerers: And the magicians of Egypt did in like manner with their enchantments: For they cast down every man his rod; and they became serpents* †.

These are supposed to have been priests of some of their false gods; and were reckoned highly skilled in art magick. According to *Artapanus*, in *Eusebius*, they were the priests of *Memphis*, fetched from thence

* Exod. vii. 9.   † Ibid 11, 12.

to oppose *Moses* *: Which there might have been time for, from his first interview with *Pharaoh*; who might have heard of *Moses's* power to work miracles, and particularly of his turning his rod into a serpent; which though done in private, might have gone abroad among the *Israelites*, and from them, among the *Egyptians*. And from what is observed above, *Pharaoh* seems to have been prepared for *Moses* by the next time he came; and his magicians might in the mean while have had opportunity for consulting their oracles, and studying the art of turning sticks into serpents, in appearance, if not in reality. Methinks they must have had some space of time for it; rather than that it should be done instantaneously.

St. *Paul* hath preserved the names of the two chief of the magicians, *Jannes* and *Jambres* †.

Whether the miracles they wrought were real, or counterfeit, hath been much doubted, and controverted. The true state of the case seems to have been this.

---

* Euseb. præp. evang. lib. ix. cap. 8. where their character, and that of *Moses*, may be seen from *Numenius* a heathen philosopher.

† 2 Tim. iii. 8.

These

These miracles, whether real or fictitious, were performed, or pretended, either by the help of some invisible powers; or by the mere art of the magicians themselves. The latter was impossible. They were above the skill or power, of any mortal to attempt. No juggler ever pretended to convert sticks into living creatures; or to a creative power of making frogs, or any reptile whatsoever; much less in such numbers, as the text implies. We have lately had among us artists in legerdemain, not inferior perhaps to any that ever existed; who yet never attempted any such feats.

It must therefore have been by the assistance of some invisible Beings, that the *Egyptian* magicians were enabled to produce such wonderful *phænomena*. For that these miracles ascribed to the magicians, were wrought immediately by the finger of God himself, is a supposition, though entertained by some, that is not to be endured.

The *Egyptian* sorcerers undoubtedly had a high opinion of the power of those gods, whose priests they were. All their credit was now at stake; and the power of their gods brought to the test. Here was a notable miracle wrought by the priest of a God, whom

whom they did not acknowledge; and if they could not equal it, their own reputation, and the honour of their gods, muſt ſuffer, and ſink to the ground. They were ordered to try what they could do. Their own intereſt, as well as credit, concurred in impelling them to do their utmoſt. They did not know how far the power of their gods extended. This was the time to prove it. We do not know, any more than they, what power any created ſpirits have. We know, indeed, becauſe we are informed, that the holy angels of God *excel in ſtrength**. We know likewiſe, that evil angels are *greater in power and might* than us feeble mortals †, and that Satan worketh *with all power, and ſigns, and lying wonders* ‡. This was the god, whom they ignorantly worſhiped, and applied to, on this occaſion: And he, we may be ſure, was determined to exert his ſtrength to the utmoſt ſtretch of it. He ſucceeded in the firſt attempt, and produced ſerpents, real, or apparent, more

---

* Pſalm ciii. 20.
† 2 Pet. ii. 11.
‡ 2 Theſ. ii. 9.

than one, from rods, as well as *Aaron*. Thus far the magicians were upon an equality with him; and even outdid him, in regard to the number. But what gave him the superiority over them was, that his serpent proved too powerful for them, and swallowed them all, whatever their numbers were. Or, as the word, יבלע, may be translated, *destroyed* them, in some manner or other; but how, is of no consequence. A man must be strangely bigotted to a notion, not to acknowledge a superiority here *.

This, however, did not discourage them from making a second, and a third experiment; and their success answered the height of their wishes. They turned water into blood; and produced frogs, as well as *Moses* and *Aaron*.

On this latter occasion, *Moses* said to *Pharaoh*, *Glory over me* †. The commentators are much perplexed, in their attempts to account for *Moses*'s addressing *Pharaoh* in these terms. But *Pharaoh* could have well gloried over *Moses*, if, by his

* See *Farmer* on Miracles, p. 447.
† Exod. viii. 9.

magicians,

magicians, and the power of his gods, he could have deftroyed the fwarms of frogs, which fo univerfally infefted the land, *even unto the king's chambers* *. This would have been fo falutary and beneficial a miracle, as would have given him a clear fuperiority over *Mofes*. And this *Mofes* fairly challenged him to do.

"You defire me to intreat the Lord, that he may take away the frogs. Order your magicians to take them away themfelves; and then *glory over me*. You will have very juft grounds for it." But this challenge produced nothing but filence. Upon which, *Mofes* afked, *When fhall I intreat for thee?* —This feems to me the moft fatisfactory account of this otherwife obfcure paffage. There fhould be a full ftop, in our tranflation, after the words, *Glory over me*, to fuit this fenfe of it.

Neither the healing of the waters turned into blood, and reftoring them to their former falubrity; nor the deftroying of the frogs, was in the power or thoughts of the magicians. The imitations of thefe miraculous plagues, which were grievous

* Pfalm cv. 30.

enough

enough already, and needed not to be multiplied, was what they were solely intent upon.

But they could *proceed no farther; and their folly was manifest unto all men**. Upon their attempting to produce lice, their usual enchantments quite failed them: And they could not help acknowledging, that this miracle was *the finger of God*; though it doth not seem to have been a greater, or more difficult one, than the production of frogs, or serpents. Some account for their ill success, from the want of any previous warning of this plague, which they had of the former ones. But their miscarriage was manifestly owing to a stop being put by the Almighty to their farther pretensions. *The illusions of art magick were put down; and their vaunting in wisdom was reproved with disgrace* †.

Moses proceeded to inflict several other miraculous plagues, which they never attempted to imitate: And, among the rest, the plague of boils, breaking out in blains upon man and beast: And the boil was upon the *magicians* ‡, as well as upon all the *Egyp-*

* 2 Tim. iii. 9.   † Wisd. xviii. 7.
‡ Exod. ix. 11.

tians.

tians. This was at once a judgement upon them for their presumption; and an evidence of their impotence to heal themselves of it.

On the other hand: Those wonderful works, surpassing any human skill or power, which the magicians did perform, are an incontestable proof of the existence of *demons*, or evil spirits, by whose aid they were enabled to perform them; and that it was not, *sine numine (lævo)* that they brought them to pass.

To account for these stupendous miracles of theirs—to reconcile them to our notions of the divine attributes—and to clear up the whole of these dark and perplexing intricacies relating to them, is the great difficulty; the solution of which, notwithstanding, I think, we need not despair of.

The Psalmist informs us, that *God cast upon the Egyptians the fierceness of his anger, wrath, and indignation, and trouble;* BY SENDING EVIL ANGELS AMONG THEM*. This is a text of great importance. It lets us into the discovery of some measures in the divine œconomy, which perhaps we

* Psalm lxxviii. 49.

might otherwise have ever continued in ignorance of.

The manner in which God cast his fierce anger and indignation upon them undoubtedly was, by visiting them with so many grievous plagues; some of which are recounted in this psalm immediately before, and some immediately after this passage; as expressions of his anger, and heavy displeasure against them. But this his sore anger, we are here told, was cast upon them, *by sending evil angels among them.* Hence, therefore, I think it clearly appears, that these were the messengers of the divine wrath; and the instruments which God Almighty was pleased to employ, in inflicting these plagues upon the Egyptians. They scared and troubled them with beasts *that passed by, hissing of serpents, monstrous apparitions, and sad visions,* with *heavy countenances,* which they exhibited to them, in *that thick darkness, which might be felt*; this being one of those plagues, by which they were much terrified, and *died with fear*; as the wise *Hebrew* describes at large in a very affecting manner*.

From the dreadful circumstances, and particular incidents, which we here meet with

* Wisd. xvii.

in the description of one of the plagues of *Egypt*, we may conclude, how inconceivably terrible they must all have been, had they been given us more in detail. The *Mosaick* history, in this, as in other respects, is very concise. The ten plagues of *Egypt* are subdivided by the *Chaldee* paraphrast on Psalm lxxviii. 49, above-mentioned, and reckoned to amount to a great number indeed: And they are imputed to evil angels. "God, says he, sent upon them two hundred and fifty plagues, in the anger of his fury, in the indignation, and expulsion, and distress, which were inflicted at that time, by the hands of evil angels."

Moses himself in his account of one of the plagues, makes express mention of *the destroyer*, by whose instrumentality it appears it was, that *he smote all the first born of the Egyptians* *. And he is followed herein by another inspired writer †. *The destroyer* is an appellation of the Devil; and it is he probably, or some other destroying angel, that is here meant. Destroying angels and destroyers, appear to have been made use of by God, on other occasions; and they are generally thought to be evil angels ‡. The

---
* Exod. xii. 23, 29, compared.
† Heb. xi. 28.
‡ 2 Sam. xxiv. 17. 1 Chr. xxi. 15. 1 Cor. x. 10.

Targum

Targum on Pſalm xii. 6, imputes *the deſtruction that waſteth at noon-day* to troops of demons. And the *Jews* afcribe many of the plagues and evils of life to wicked ſpirits.

The Lord of the creation may employ any of his creatures, good or bad, as inſtruments of his will; whether it be for judgment, for correction, or for mercy. He admits of the ſervices, the prophecies, and the miracles of wicked men. Such was *Balaam*; and ſuch were thoſe, who ſaid, *Lord, Lord, Have we not propheſied in thy name? And in thy name caſt out Devils? And in thy name done many wonderful works** ?

Why therefore might not God make uſe of the miniſtry of evil angels, in inflicting the plagues of *Egypt* ?

Now admitting this to have been the caſe, we can from hence account for their ſucceſs, in turning the waters into blood, and in producing frogs, a ſecond time; as theſe miracles were no more than a repetition of what they had been empowered to perform before; the power of repeating them having not been withdrawn from

---

* Matt. vii. 22. Compare Jo. xi. 51. 1 Cor. xiii. 2.

them. And, as for their turning the rods into serpents; this was permitted, as it terminated in God's glory; into which it was converted.

When the plague of lice was inflicted, the magicians attempted to *bring forth lice likewise, by their inchantments*; flattering themselves with hopes of the like success, as they had met with on the former occasions.

But when, upon finding themselves disappointed, they acknowledged to *Pharaoh*, that *this was the finger of God*; this implies that they looked upon the former miracles of *Moses*, as having been performed by the help of the same powers, with those, by whom they knew they themselves had been enabled to contend with him: Nor did they know till now, but that he, and *Aaron* might have been magicians, like themselves; and might have gone the same way to work; as the same spirits were instrumental in producing the same miracles. By this test they were convinced, that these their gods were inferior Beings; who, on this occasion, acted in subserviency to the supreme power and will of the Almighty Creator, and Lord of heaven and earth; whom,

whom, it seems, they had not lost all knowledge of.

The plagues of *Egypt* were all miraculous. The imitations of them by the magicians, as far as they went, were in all appearance, and according to the scripture-account, miraculous likewise. And as God sometimes thinks fit to make use of, or permit, the worst of Beings to work miracles: So he can put a stop to them, when he pleases; and can prevent, or defeat, any impostures that are attempted, under the umbrage of them; and frustrate their ill effects: As we find he did, in disabling the magicians from proceeding to perform the miracle of turning the dust into lice; or any others.

Most probably, the instrumentality of those evil angels having been abused before by them, was likewise laid aside, in the performance of the remaining miracles; excepting that, in which it is expressly said, the *destroyer* was employed.

Maimonides suspected, that all miracles might be wrought by the power of magick and incantation*.

---

* Maim. de Fund. Leg. cap. viii. sect. 1.

But if so, I know not of what signification he could think the miracles of God could be. No miracle, I am fully satisfied, can be performed, by any other Being, or any other means; but by his appoinment, or permission, who is at the helm of the whole universe, and guides every movement of it.

No portion of Scripture wanted more to be cleared up, than this relating to the rival powers of the magicians. Many solutions of the difficulty have been offered: But none, I think, that hath entirely removed it. This attempt presents the whole in a new light; and, I flatter myself, it is the true one: But of that the impartial reader is to judge.

We have seen to what a height magical arts were carried in *Egypt*. It was natural for the *Israelites*, and almost unavoidable, from their continuance in that country for so many ages, to catch the contagion, and to imbibe the ill principles and practices of their masters: For the correcting of which, many of the laws of *Moses* appear to have been especially calculated. Among others, we find, there were very severe laws

laws made against witches, wizards, and necromancers.

These were capital offenders. *Thou shalt not suffer a witch to live* *. *A man, or woman, that hath a familiar spirit, or that is a wizard, shall surely be put to death* †. The consulting of such was highly offensive to God; and was punished with extermination. *The soul that turneth after such as have familiar spirits, and after wizards, to go a whoring after them; I will even set my face against that soul; and will cut him off from among my people* ‡. *There shall not be found among you one that useth divination, or an observer of times, or an enchanter, or a witch: Or a charmer, or a consulter with familiar spirits, or a wizard, or a necromancer* ‖. Where we see there is special provision repeatedly made against all these nefarious and infernal practices. They were all abominations, for which *Egypt* was so infamous; and for which likewise, we are

* Exod. xxii. 18.
† Lev. xx. 27.
‡ Ver. 6. See ch. xix. 26, 31.
‖ Deut. xviii. 10, 11.

informed,

informed, the Lord drove the *Canaanites* out of the land *.

The word, which our translators render *a familiar spirit*, in the original is אוב; for which translation we are told, " they are not " wholly to be condemned." If they are to be condemned in any measure, a better translation ought to be offered. Instead of that, it is remarked, that the word denotes only a *bottle-bellied* person, and insinuated, that no more is signified by it †. But a poor creature must be very unfortunate; and the laws of *Moses* must have been very whimsical, as well as tyrannical, to condemn such a wretch to be stoned to death, for the unfavourable make of his body. The severity of the punishment evinces the reality of the possession. And this rendering, which was introduced by the last translators, I think, is a very happy one, and conveys the proper idea, in as clear and becoming terms, as any antient or modern one whatsoever.

The word is translated ἐγγαςριμυθος by the LXX. ten times. The *Syriack* trans-

* Deut. xviii. 12.
† See *Farmer* on Miracles, p. 273.

lates

lates by a word that anſwers to *a ſorcerer.* The *Arabick*, by a word ſignifying *a magician*; which is much the ſame. The *Vulgate* renders *Pytho*; in which it is followed by ſome later tranſlations. Among our old Engliſh tranſlators, *Coverdale* renders it, *a ſoythſayer*; *Tindal, one that worketh with a ſpryte*; and *Matthews* and *Cranmer* tranſlate much in the ſame manner.—*A familiar ſpirit* ſignifies an inmate of that kind, or an intimate attendant upon one; that is poſſeſſed by, or addicted to it.

This tranſlation, it is true, is a little paraphraſtical; if the gentleman, who objects to it, will be pleaſed to improve upon it, he will be entitled to thanks.

But, if he really wants to know the full import of the original word, let him conſult *Fuller*, or the learned *Selden*, with *Beyer's* additions; in which he will find, that the word, אוֹב, bears five different ſenſes in Scripture; and of theſe, that which he repreſents it in, is the loweſt*.

The *Pythoneſs* was inflated by the poſſeſſing demon, as the original name imports;

---

* Vide Seldeni Syntagma de Teraphim, cum additamentis Beyeri. Et Fulleri Miſc. Sacra, lib. I. cap. xvi.

and resembled a pregnant woman: And hence, I doubt not, arose the corrupt opinion of old, that the demons cohabited with females of the human race, and had issue by them. Which it is not improbable, that these *Pythonesses* often had, though not by demons*.

When they were seized, and rapt by the demons, they fell into fits of raving and frenzy; in which they lost themselves, not knowing, what they said, or did, as *Origen* describes them †: And this answers to the description of several of the gospel demoniacks.

We find in the *Hebrew* republick some early instances of the people's proneness to false worship and idolatry; with which divination and magick were connected of course. *Gideon made an ephod—and all Israel went a whoring after it: Which thing became a snare unto Gideon, and to his house* ‡. Whatever the nature of this *Ephod* was, it

---

* Thus our prophet *Merlin* was fathered upon an *Incubus*, to cloak the shame of the nun, his mother; who was supposed to have been impregnated by the *Roman* general.

† Origen contra Celsum, lib. vii. p. 333.

‡ Judges viii. 27.

was egregiously misapplied, and made the instrument of the people's infidelity to their God, whom they had been espoused and devoted to. *As soon as Gideon was dead, the children of Israel turned again from God,* became more open idolaters, *and went a whoring after Baalim, and made Baal-berith their God**. It would be endless to recount the names of all the false gods, whose worship the *Israelites* adopted, and were, more or less, addicted to, through all the periods of their republick, till the *Assyrian* captivity of the ten tribes; and the *Babylonish* captivity of the two remaining ones; into both which they were all driven for their idolatry; and by which the latter were at length reclaimed from it.

Though they had from the beginning a divine oracle, and inspired prophets, to consult and advise with; yet were they very prone at all times to betake themselves to those that had familiar spirits, and to wizards, and diviners. This rendered their offence the more inexcuseable, as they addicted themselves to those practices, in disdain and despight of those better and more certain

* Chap. ix. 38.

lights; which were held out to them, in opposition to those false and delusive ones, from which they were intended to draw them.

To proceed in pointing out some particulars. Agreeably to what hath been observed already, we read, that *God sent an evil spirit* between *Abimilech* and the men of *Shichem*; for no good purpose we may be sure, as appears by the context, which their attachment to false gods subjected them to*.

Micah had an house of gods, in which were *a graven image, and a molten image*; and he *made an ephod and Teraphim; and consecrated one of his sons, who became his priest* †. Here we find these *Teraphim* again; and they appear to have been in such frequent use, and general estimation, that they occur no less than fifteen times in the Old Testament. They are supposed to have been a kind of *Talismans*, by which future events were prognosticated: Or *amulets* kept in families, and by single persons, for the cure of distempers, and protection from harm ‡.

* Judges ix. 23. 27.
† Chap. xxviii. 4, 5, 6.
‡ Vide Selden & Fuller, ubi suprà.

From the scripture accounts of them, I take them, with regard to their construction, to have been none other than small images of their *Lares*, or houshold gods; which were supposed to have some virtue for that purpose.

Witches and wizards became so numerous, and the practice of consulting them was become so pernicious in the time of *Saul*, that this prince found it necessary *to put those that had familiar spirits, and the wizards, out of the land; and to cut them off**. Notwithstanding this, he soon afterwards found himself in such a streight, that when the Lord would not answer him, either by dreams, or by *Urim*, or by prophets; he was tempted to have recourse to a woman, that had a familiar spirit, to enquire of her; and employ her to bring up the ghost of *Samuel*, to be consulted with by him, in his distress †.

Bishop *Patrick* supposes it was an evil spirit that personated *Samuel's* ghost; and that he had been employed by God to declare his mind to *Saul*, concerning his

* 1 Sam. xxxiii. 3. 9.
† Ib. ver. 7.

approaching

approaching fate; agreeably to what is observed above, that God may make use of the instrumentality of evil spirits, for wise purposes of his providence. And agreeably likewise to what we have seen concerning the artifices of these evil spirits, in personating the souls of the dead in possessions.

Saul's offence, in asking counsel of one that had a familiar spirit, and not enquiring of the Lord, was so great, that God is said to have slain him on that account *.

This was but putting the law abovementioned in execution against him—that law which he had lately put in execution himself, against those that had familiar spirits.

It is true, the Lord had once refused to answer him; and therefore, in disgust, or despair, he turned aside, and had recourse to forbidden counsels. But had he persevered in his request, God might at length have been prevailed upon to satisfy his enquiries. Though *he answered him not that day* †; he might have answered him the morrow. It was *Saul's* hasty and impatient spirit, on this occasion, as upon others ‡; particularly, in not waiting but perhaps a few minutes longer for *Samuel's* arrival, be-

---

* 1 Chron. x. 14.   † 1 Sam. xiv. 37.   ‡ Ver. 19.

fore

fore he offered sacrifice, that proved his ruin*.

Saul himself was at times troubled with an evil spirit. *When the spirit of the Lord departed from Saul, an evil spirit from the Lord troubled him* †.

Saul had once a good setting out; and had he constantly followed the guidance of God's Holy Spirit, he could never have miscarried; but would have prospered, and been as successful as *Joshua, Gideon, Jephtha* ‡, and other worthies were, who went before him under the same divine leader. But *Saul* having more than once disregarded the spirit of the Lord ||; He then, and not till then, forsook him likewise, and abandoned him to the incursions of the evil spirit §.

This is called *an evil spirit from the Lord*; as being commissioned by God to execute his judgments upon this wicked prince; and to inflict this punishment upon him;

* 1 Sam. xiii. 8.
† Chap. xvi. 14
‡ Deut. xxxiv. 9.
|| Judg. iii. 10.—vi. 34.—xi. 29.
§ Com. 1 Sam. xiii. 13.—xiv. 37.—xv. 11. with ch. xvi. 14.

whereby he was, at times, terrified, and troubled, and thrown into fits of frenzy and distraction.

Josephus represents *Saul's* case as demoniacal; for that after the departure of the good spirit, he fell εις παθη δεινα και δαιμονια, into demoniacal passions; and had, απο των δαιμονων ταραχην, perturbations from demons. And that he was taken with fits and fancies of suffocation, like a demoniack. And he makes *Jonathan* remind *Saul*, that it was *David* who cured him of his dark splenetick fits; and drove the evil spirit from him *.

All the fathers are agreed, that *Saul's* case was demoniacal. I take it to have been a mixt case; partly natural and partly demoniacal. The best account I can give of it is as follows.

Saul, having been informed by *Samuel*, that God had determined to deprive him, and his heirs, of the kingdom; because of his disobedience and rebellion; in not hearkening to the voice of the prophet, on two several occasions; was so deeply affected with the misfortune; and so enraged at

* Antiq. lib. vi. cap. ix. 13.

himself for being the sole cause of it; that whenever the thoughts of it occurred to him, he at length grew quite distracted, for the time. And as it often happens, that when a man is displeased with his own conduct, he is apt to vent his passion upon other people; and even sometimes, upon those that are nearest, and dearest to him: So *Saul*, in those fits of frenzy, often sought to kill *David*: And *Jonathan* too narrowly escaped the effects of his fury.

As he was become so outrageous, at times, and so much to be dreaded by all about him; it was every one's business to keep him in good humour, as much as possible. For which purpose, his courtiers thought musick might be of service to calm and assuage his passions: And *David* having been introduced to court, as being well-skilled in the harp, his playing upon it proved of great service in this respect, and relieved him much, as occasion required.

The spirit of the Lord having departed from *Saul*, the evil spirit, who watches all opportunities of falling upon us, and never misses any advantage he can find against us, struck in with *Saul's* weakness, and heightened his disorder. For it hath been well observed, ferved, "That it is probable evil fpirits lay hold of the indifpofition of the body, to diftrefs the foul, and infult human reafon, by occupying the imagination unnaturally—That diforders of reafon are often the effects of, and attended by, this unnatural occupation, by fpirits, who have not power enough to invade the quiet of the foul, till its origin be previoufly difordered.—And that the region of memory is darkened by this means."

It is very probable likewife, that when men caft off the fear of God, and prove rebellious againft him, he withdraws his protection; and "takes off the curb, that reftains the power of evil fpirits: And they may then terrify the foul with unpleafing fights, vifible only to thofe, againft whom they are thus let out, as the poet tells us, *Pentheus* and *Oreftes* were purfued by vifible furies, the one for facrifice, the other for parricide." This is agreeable to the defcription relative to the plagues of *Egypt*, in Wifd. xvii, above taken notice of. I wifh that whole chapter were here again perufed, and compared with what is obferved above.

"It is certain, as our christian philoso-
"pher adds, that these disorders of rea-
"son appear after grief, love, or some
"great disappointment, have discomposed
"the brain *."

It is probable *Saul's* case was something similar to those above mentioned from the poets, and comes under the like description. At least, that it was not of so slight a nature, as the author of the Essay on Demoniacks makes it to be †.

David did not play on the harp to charm the evil spirit; but to calm and compose the disturbed imagination, and allay the natural disorder; upon which the man being restored to his right mind, *the spirit of the Lord* returned and chased away *the evil spirit* from him ‡.

It is hinted above, That disorders of the understanding often affect the memory. This might have been *Saul's* case, in having lost all knowledge of *David*; who had been so often in his presence and company;

---

* Enquiry into the human Soul. vol. ii. p. 144. 148.
† P. 174.
‡ 1 Sam. xvi. 14. xix. 23.

whom he had admitted into such intimacies with him; and was so fond of, that he made him his armour-bearer, and greatly delighted in his musick*.

If we take this clue along with us, it will help us to unravel the inconsistences which otherwise appear in this part of *Saul's* history; without supposing any transposition in it, as some do. *Saul's* loss of memory might have been the result of a disordered, and impaired mind, among other instances of it. As for *Abner's* being a stranger to *David's* person; that is sufficiently accounted for, from supposing him to have been absent in the wars; when *David* happened to be at court.

To pass on now to some other cases. *God put an evil spirit in the mouth of all Ahab's prophets; to the number of four hundred*; in order to intice him to go up, and fall at *Ramoth Gilead* †. These were the prophets of the grove, who were just so many in number; and were maintained by *Jezebel* ‡. The measure of this wicked prince's iniquities being filled up; and having made

---

* 1 Sam. xvi. 21, 22, 23.
† 2 Chr. xviii. 19.
‡ 1 Kings xviii. 19.

him

him ripe for destruction; God thought fit to bring it about in this manner, by suffering him to be misled by those false prophets, in whom he had always so much confided: But notwithstanding he forewarned him of it, by the mouth of his own true prophet *Micaiah*; that he might have it in his power to avoid it.

This is represented by way of vision; in which it is said, that *Micaiah* saw God sitting on his throne, and all the host of heaven standing by him; the good angels on his right hand, and the bad ones on his left; to shew the deliberate purpose of the Almighty to punish *Ahab* in this manner; and at the same time to indicate to us, that he hath in fact, at all times, ministers of his will, in readiness to execute it, as well in punishing the disobedient, as in rewarding his obedient servants.

The event verified the prediction, and confirmed the truth of the information which it contained: But I presume it is not necessary to suppose, that *Micaiah* had in reality any such vision; for that he himself, in order to undeceive *Ahab*, if possible, might have contrived this innocent, and well-meant fiction; to inform him, in this striking manner, that it was by the determinate council of the Almighty, that he gave him up, to be infatuated by the delusion of evil spirits; and to be misled by them into his own ruin; as a just judgment upon him, for his great and manifold transgressions.

At the same time we may observe, that the strong expressions in this passage, and indeed the whole purport of it, may serve to confirm the doctrine above laid down; and proved by other instances; that God makes use of the instrumentality of evil spirits, to carry on the designs of his providence in the government of the world.

We may observe here, by the way, that *Micaiah* was not without a spice of the courtier in him. He, as well as the other prophets, at first prophesied smooth things to the monarch. But upon being adjured to say nothing but the truth, he soon altered his note; and the true prediction being extorted from him, deserved the greater regard *.

Ahaziah, the son of *Ahab*, was not cured of his father's attachment to idolatry; nor of his confidence in false gods. In a dan-

* 1 Kings xxii. 22. 2 Chr. xviii. 19.

gerous hurt which he had by a fall; inftead of applying to the God of *Ifrael* for help, or enquiring of his word, by the mouth of his prophet *Elijah*, he fent to confult *Baalzebub*, the God of *Ekron*, a city of the *Philiftines*; for which he was feverely reproved by the man of God, who likewife denounced his death; which came to pafs accordingly; together with the divine judgment, inflicted upon two companies of his murderous meffengers by a fire from Heaven; which was at once a demonftration of the inability of the falfe God, in whom he trufted, to reftore him to health; of the fuperiority of the true God, whom he difdained; and likewife of the triumph of his poor fervant, a naked man, over his God's enemies, and his own, to the number of a hundred and fifty, by deftroying fome, and humbling the reft [*]; to the confufion of thofe who confulted falfe gods, and all idolaters.

The practice of applying to wizards, and fuch as had familiar fpirits, continued in the following reigns; and is taken notice of, and reproved, by the prophets who lived in

[*] 2 Kings, i. 2.

these times. *Isaiah*, in the reign of *Ahaz*, thus remonstrates against them: *When they shall say unto you, seek unto them that have familiar spirits, and unto wizards that peep, and that mutter; should not a people seek unto their God* * ?

This is a just description of these magicians, who never spake plainly; but whispered and murmured in their incantations. The word translated *peep* is not here to be understood in its common acceptation. In the original, it is supposed to signify the uttering of a slender, faint voice, like the chirping of birds: And that is the sense in the translation; from the latin *pipio*, which signifies the small chirping note of young birds. Both the words, *peep*, and *mutter*, denote the obscurity of the heathen oracles, as well in the utterance, as in the sense of them. None of them spake with a natural voice.

Hence, by the way, we may observe, that there was a great difference between the note of these oracles, when they were consulted by their votaries; and when the *demons* that delivered them were approached

* Isaiah viii. 19.

by our Saviour, and spake in the possessed. They did not then whisper, in a slender, still accent; but they were forced *to cry out with a loud voice*; of which we meet with many instances in the gospels*. And this I doubt not was meant by way of contrast, to convince mankind of the difference between these feeble, and scarce intelligible sounds, which they made of their own accord, when unconstrained, upon their being consulted; and those vociferations, which were extorted from them, when they were compelled to expose themselves, and quit their usurped possessions.

The LXX understood these mutterers to have been such as spake out of the belly, thence called ventriloquists, and by them translated Εγγαςριμυθυς: And again, in this same verse, Οἱ εκ της κοιλιας φωνυσιν †.

The same prophet, in describing the confusion of *Egypt*, says, *they shall seek to the idols, and to the charmers, and to them that*

---

* See Mark i. 23. Luke iv. 33. viii. 28. And Acts viii. 7.

† The Scholiast on *Aristophanes* gives the following just definition of ventriloquists, Ουτος, ὡς εγγαςρ μυθος λεγεται Αθηνησι τ'αληθη, μαντευομενος δι'ενυπαρχοντος αυτω δαιμονος.

have familiar spirits, and to the wizards * This is in character. We have seen how much the *Egyptians* were addicted to sorcery and magick: And we here see how closely these arts, and those that practised them, were connected with idols and idolatry, being here mentioned together. The LXX here translate, τες εκ της γης φωνουν]ας, και τους εγ[ασριμυθους, speaking out of the ground, and divining out of the belly.

Again, *Thou shalt be brought down, and shalt speak out of the ground; and thy speech shall be low, out of the dust; and thy voice shall be, as one that hath a familiar spirit, out of the ground; and thy speech shall whisper out of the dust*: plainly and expressly alluding to the low and obscure muttering of the heathen oracles; which is here dwelt upon, and repeated no less than four times with very little variety of expression; in order the more effectually to expose them. They who delivered these oracles sat over the mouth of a cavern, whence the voice seemed to come.

Chaldea and *Babylon* are proverbially notorious for their attachment to magick, and

* Isaiah xix. 3.

judicial astrology; insomuch that those nefarious arts are supposed to have originally sprung from that country. The prophet doth not fail to denounce God's judgments upon it, *for the multitude of its sorceries; and for the great abundance of its enchantments. Stand now with thine enchantments, and with the multitude of thy sorceries; wherein thou hast laboured from thy youth—Let now the astrologers, the star-gazers, the monthly prognosticators stand up, and save thee from those things that shall come upon thee* *.

The wicked King *Manasses* used *enchantments, and witchcraft, and dealt with familiar spirits, and wizards. He wrought much wickedness in the sight of the Lord, after the abomination of the heathens, to provoke him to anger;* of which these were instances.

He was a great idolater, and *made his son pass through the fire;* by which learned men understand, that he offered him in sacrifice to *Moloch*, as was the practice of the *Canaanites*, and other heathen nations; and then raked into the bowels of the victim, to divine, or consult the god by; which was

* Isaiah xlvii. 9, 12, 13. Vide Fulleri Misc. Sacra, lib. i. cap. 16.

the

the moſt inhuman and abominable of all magical rites *.

The good king *Joſiah* found it highly neceſſary to make a reformation. He *put away the workers with familiar ſpirits; and the wizards; and the images, and the idols, and all the other abominations, that were ſpied in the land of Judah and Jeruſalem; that he might perform the words of the law* †, above taken notice of. *He defiled Topheth, that no man might* make his children *paſs through the fire to Moloch*; and extirpated idolatry in all its branches; with which magical rites were conſtantly intermixed. From the large and particular account which we have of his zeal in purging the land of all theſe abominations, it appears how univerſally the corruption had ſpread, and prevailed in the preceding reigns.

Jeremiah, who lived in the reign of *Joſiah*, condemns the falſe prophets; and ranks them with ſorcerers and enchanters. *The Lord ſaid unto me, the prophets propheſy lies in my name—They propheſy unto you a falſe viſion, and divination* ‡. *Hearken not ye unto*

---

* 2 Kings xxi. 6.   2 Chron. xxxiii. 6.
† 2 Kings xxiii. 24.   ‡ Jer. xiv. 14.

your

your prophets, nor your diviners; nor to your dreamers; nor to your enchanters; nor to your sorcerers *. And again, *Let not your prophets, and your diviners, that be in the midst of you, deceive you* †. Because they spake peace to them, when there was no peace; and flattered them with security and deliverance from the King of *Babylon,* which they had not the least grounds for.

In *Ezekiel's* description of the king of *Babylon's* approach to *Jerusalem,* when he came to besiege it, we have an account of the method of divination by arrows; a superstitious usage said to be still observed by some idolatrous people in the east. *The King of Babylon stood at the parting of the way, at the head of the two ways, to use divination. He made his arrows bright: He consulted with images: He looked in the liver. At his right hand was the divination for Jerusalem, to appoint captains; to open the mouth in the slaughter; to lift up the voice with shouting; to appoint battering rams against the gates; to cast a mount, and to build a fort: And it shall be unto them as a false divination in their sight* ‡.

* Jer. xxvii. 9. † Ch. xxix. 8.
‡ Ezekiel xxi. 21, 22, 23.

It

It is observed above, that the *Chaldeans* were much addicted to magick and astrology. In the book of *Daniel*, the professors of those sciences are called *Chaldeans*. *The King commanded to call the magicians, and the astrologers, and the sorcerers, and the* Chaldeans ; *for to shew the King his dream* *. And in the context they are several times called *Chaldeans* only; by which this seems to be a general name, inclusive of all the rest †. The King of *Babylon* constantly retained a number of these dealers in infernal rites and mysteries ; and his attention to them appears in an institution which he established for the maintenance and instruction of some choice youths of the nobility of *Israel* likewise in this learning, and in the tongue of the *Chaldeans* ; to whom, by the way, *God gave such knowledge and skill in all true learning and wisdom, that the King*, upon enquiry, *found them ten times better*, in this respect, *than all the magicians and astrologers that were in all his realm* ‡.

God was pleased to give *Nebuchadnezzar* an opportunity of bringing the skill of these

* Daniel ii. 2.   † Ibid. viii. 5. 10.
‡ Daniel i. 4, 17, 20.

pretenders

pretenders to *wisdom, falsely so called*, to the test; by certain dreams, which had escaped his memory; and which they were required to *make known unto him*, together *with the interpretation*. But this was what neither they, nor indeed any mere mortals, as they observed, could pretend to. *But Daniel had understanding in all visions and dreams* *. And the God of Heaven, who *revealeth secrets, revealed this secret to him* †.

It was an antient opinion, That not only private persons had their guardian angels; but that empires likewise had their tutelar *genii*, or deities, presiding over them, and taking them under their peculiar protection. This opinion is countenanced by scripture. We read in this book of the Princes of *Persia* and *Grecia*; who are by most commentators supposed to have been evil spirits; and who were supposed to bear great sway over those heathen kingdoms; and to set them against the people of God. In defence of whom, *Michael*, one of the chief princes, elsewhere called the Arch-angel, is mentioned as interposing in their defence, and *standing for*

* Daniel i. 17. † Daniel ii. 18, 19.

*the children of God's people**. *Gabriel*, another holy angel, is mentioned, as the appointed interpreter of *Daniel's* vision †. We here likewise read of *Mahuzzim, the God of forces, a strange God*, by which is always meant a false one; who should have much honour paid him ‡.

We likewise read in *Zechariah* of *Joshua, the high priest, standing before the angel of the Lord, and Satan standing at his right hand to resist him:* Whose boldness was so great, that *the Lord said unto Satan, The Lord rebuke thee, O Satan* §.

Now in whatever manner this sight was exhibited to the prophet, whether in reality, or perhaps only in vision; it nevertheless is grounded upon the reality of this wicked spirit's existence; and is suitable to his general character. The four spirits of the heavens, which go forth from standing before the Lord of all the earth ‖, are supposed to be the angels, which presided over the four great monarchies.

* Ch. x. 13, 20. xii. 1.   † Ch. viii. 16. ix. 2.
‡ Ch. xi. 38, 39.   § Zech. iii. 1, 2.
‖ Ch. vi. 5.

But what is of special notice, there is in this book express mention of *unclean spirits*; a term, which occurs no where else in the Old Testament. And it is mentioned by way of prophecy; and that prophecy was evidently fulfilled by our Saviour. *And it shall come to pass in that day, saith the Lord of hosts, that I will cut off the names of the idols out of the land; and they shall no more be remembered: And also, I will cause the prophets, and the unclean spirit to pass out of the land**.

This prophecy commences at verse 9, of the foregoing chapter, and all the events foretold in it are pointed out for having their accomplishment at one and the same period of time, by an expression often repeated in it, *In that day*, that is, in the gospel age. Thus particularly—*In that day*—*I will pour out upon the house of David, and upon the inhabitants of Jerusalem, the spirit of grace and supplications:* Parallel to which is that prophecy of *Joel*, *I will pour out my spirit upon all flesh* †. This prophecy, we are taught by St. *Peter*, was fulfilled by the descent of the Holy Ghost upon the Apostles, at the

* Ch. xiii. 2. † Joe. 28.

day of *Pentecost**. This event therefore was an accomplishment likewife of this its parallel prophecy in *Zechariah*. I will pour upon the house of *David*, and upon the inhabitants of *Jerusalem*, the spirit of grace, and of supplications—*and they shall look upon me, whom they have pierced*. This latter prophecy, St. *John* teaches us, was fulfilled at our Saviour's crucifixion †. *In that day*, again—In that same day, *there shall be a fountain opened to the* forementioned *house of David, and inhabitants of Jerusalem, for sin and for uncleanness*—for the expiation of sin by the blood of the lamb; and for the washing away of all moral impurities, by the graces of the Holy Spirit; and by the purity of the gospel precepts. *And it shall come to pass* in that day likewise, in that age, and none other, *saith the Lord of Hosts*, whose promise cannot fail, *that I will cut off the names of the idols out of the land*. I will effectually destroy idolatry, and abolish the very names of the idols; and their memorial shall perish with them; *and they shall no more be remembered*. This being the general

---

* Acts ii. 16, 17. † John xix. 37.

purport

purport of the christian dispensation, to destroy and eradicate all false worship, and to establish the belief, worship, and service of the only true God, in its stead. And even independently of christianity, this prediction may be literally understood of the extirpating of idolatry *out of the land* of *Judah*; in which it never once got any footing since the gospel age. And also, as it is added in reference to the same day still, *I will cause the prophets, and the unclean spirit to pass out of the land.* By the prophets being here joined with the unclean spirit, must be meant false prophets, which abounded so much before the gospel age; but which were to be suppressed at its appearance. And the context determines accordingly; which says, that *when any shall yet prophesy*, he shall be reckoned to *speak lies in the name of the Lord*; and be sentenced to be put to death; his nearest kindred being the first to put the sentence in execution, according to the law of *Moses**.

Now as all the preceding parts of this prophecy clearly relate to the gospel age, and have been fulfilled in it; it unavoidably follows, that the remaining prediction—*I*

---

* Deut. xii. 8, 9.

will cause the unclean spirit to pass out of the land—must have its accomplishment in it likewise, if it be accomplished at all. And here we cannot fail to find it fulfilled in the many open expulsions of *unclean spirits*, often under that very denomination; as well as often under many others, recorded in the gospel; all in confirmation of each other; insomuch that there is no room to mistake, or evade the truth and reality of the accomplishment, in its most obvious and literal sense *.

From this view of the passages relating to demonology, and demoniacal possessions, in the prophetical, as well as historical parts of the Old Testament, we see there is surely *some* foundation for the doctrine of possessions in it; contrary to what the author of the essay is pleased to assert; and that it received the sanction of the prophets of the Old, as well as New Testament. We have seen some direct instances of real possessions: many allusions to them; and many collateral proofs from the doctrines relating to

---

* See Twells' answer to Sykes' Enquiry about demoniacks, p. 70. See likewise Micah x. 12. and Nahum iii. 4. relating to this subject.

evil

evil spirits. The having of familiar spirits particularly, implies possession, or at least obsession, in the very term; we have seen likewise frequent mention of magicians, sorcerers, wizards; many, if not all, of whom were possessed; or at least under the influence of evil spirits. And though some of the above passages do not relate immediately to possessions, yet they relate to subjects in connection with them, and from which possessions may, by fair inference, be proved.

Notwithstanding all this, our author peremptorily declares, That " with regard to the prophets of the Old Testament, they stand clear from all suspicion of countenancing the doctrine of real possessions. It is not pretended, says he, that they ever expressly taught it. In all their writings, as, he adds, no traces of it are to be found; no mention of a single instance of reputed possession; nor any allusion to it*."

These are bold assertions; but they are only assertions. To make them good, all the proofs here produced, or at least the greatest part, and most considerable of them

---

* See Essay on Demoniacks, p. 173.

ought

ought to have been disproved. But nothing of this hath been attempted. They are all in a manner overlooked: But they are here brought into view; and I doubt not will have their weight with the impartial reader.

To condemn scripture doctrines thus in the lump—to banish them out of the scriptures, and to over-rule scripture itself, in so decretorial a manner, sounds more like the language of the council of *Trent*, than that of a protestant divine. The only case in the Old Testament that he thinks fit to take notice of, is that of *Saul*; against which what is observed above, I trust, will be a sufficient antidote.

I have not yet done with the demonology of the Old Testament. No where do we find such an account of demonism, as in the book of *Job:* Where the chief of all wicked spirits appears in so open, undisguised, and daring a manner, even in the presence of his great Creator: Which is sufficient to convince us, how bold and intrepid, how busy and restless an enemy of mankind he is—That he is eager to accuse, and undaunted in his attempts, upon the virtue of the most perfect and upright of the sons of men; and hath various ways of tempting them to

transgress

transgress their duty—That God sometimes thinks fit to permit his having great sway in the world for this purpose—That men are liable to be deprived by him of all their outward possessions; and are not safe from him even in their persons; having power to inflict bodily diseases upon them; and to deprive them of every thing that is nearest, and dearest to them—That his malice is unsatiable, and knows no bounds—But that notwithstanding, in the exercise of it, he is under certain restraints and limitations—That he is amenable for his conduct; and under the strict government of the Almighty.

All this we have in the first and second chapters of the book of *Job*. The *Jews* were convinced of these truths, if not otherwise, yet from hence, as this book made part of the canon of their scriptures: And *Maimonides* expressly acknowledges, that *Satan* was the cause of all *Job's* sufferings, both in his substance, and body*. And this book, being constantly in their hands, helped to facilitate their belief of our Saviour's temptations; to which the trials of

---

* Maim. More Nevoch. lib. iii. cap. 22.

Job bear so great an analogy, that I think the history of the one cannot be destroyed, without impairing that of the other likewise. The doctrine however here contained is the same, in whatever view the book is taken.

There was a day, on which the Sons of God, the holy angels, as is supposed, *came to present themselves before the Lord;* to give an account of their ministry; and to receive his commands. Where we are told, That *Satan came also among them**. Hence we learn, that the sovereign Lord of the universe hath his ministers, whom he employs in the government of it—That he calls them to an account of their administrations, in their respective offices and departments—That he hath stated times and seasons, on which he convenes them for this purpose—That he not only " ordains and constitutes the services of his holy angels, as well as men, in a wonderful order," but that he makes use of the fallen angels likewise, in executing his will; and that the Devil himself is accountable to him for his conduct, and subject to his controul. But notwith-

* Job ii. 2.

standing

standing the confummate impudence of this moſt daring of all created beings, it ſeems moſt probable, that he did not intrude of himſelf into the divine preſence; but that he was convened to appear among the reſt of the miniſtring ſpirits, to give an account of his actions and behaviour; in ſome manner analogous to the appearances of us mortals, before the tribunals of our ſuperiors here on earth, allowing for the difference ariſing from the different natures of ſpiritual and corporeal creatures, and between heavenly and earthly tribunals.

Immediately upon *Satan's* appearance before the Lord, God demanded of him, whence he came. To which he was obliged to own, he came from traverſing the earth, for the ſake of making his obſervations on mankind, in order to find out ſuch of them as were fit to be made a prey of.

Upon this, the Lord aſks him, as he was ſo narrow an inſpector into the manners of men, whether he had conſidered his ſervant *Job*; whoſe moral and religious character was ſuch, as he knew to be irreproachable; and he ſeemed to glory in it, as being proof againſt the aſſaults of his enemy.

The subtle adversary insinuated, that the virtue of this boasted saint was mercenary, and his piety all precarious and hypocritical; founded on his security and affluence: For if God would but permit him to be deprived of his great wealth, he should soon see how impious a wretch he would prove.

God, willing to try the virtue of his servant by adversity, as well as prosperity, left all his substance at the will of this unmerciful enemy; who instantly brought one calamity so quick after another upon him, that in one day he found himself stript of all his substance of every kind: And to crown all, he was deprived by him of a numerous family of children grown up, and happily settled in the world.

He first brought the *Sabeans*, or wild *Arabs*, known to have always been a thievish people, to drive away his oxen and asses, and to murder his servants. No sooner had *Job* been informed of this loss; but in comes another account of his sheep and shepherds having been blasted, and destroyed by lightning; caused likewise by *Satan*, having it seems been licensed to bear rule over the elements, for this purpose. He then raised the *Chaldeans* to fall upon the camels for plunder; and to carry them away, killing

his

his servants likewise. And to complete his calamity, this prince of the power of the air raised a great storm, or whirlwind; and directed it against the four corners of the house, in which all *Job's* children were assembled, and securely feasting together; levelled it with the ground, and buried them all in the ruins.

All these heavy shocks, coming so thick, one upon the heels of the other, did not shake the firmness of this good man's virtue; but produced in him the most perfect resignation. In all this *Job* sinned not, nor charged God foolishly.

These severe trials, thus manfully gone through, only served to enrage the malicious adversary the more; and having obtained power over the person of this upright man, after he had ruined him in his fortune and family, he pursued his unprovoked and unremitted rage against him, by inflicting a most loathsome disease upon him; and smiting him with sore boils, from the sole of his foot, unto his crown. And to add to the plague, he excited another tempter, the wife of his bosom, to urge him to *curse God, and die*. But in all this, did not *Job* sin with his lips.

If

If a man of so perfect a character was thus obnoxious to the assaults of *Satan*, and to be vexed by him with all his storms; what have others to apprehend from this their spiritual enemy; who are not so well entitled to the divine protection? God be praised that his power is limited, and hath its bounds that it cannot pass.

It doth not become us to speculate about this dialogue between God and the Devil. We are to take the facts as they are represented to us, in the word of God; which in this passage gives us the greatest insight into the nature and character of this accursed spirit; beyond what we have elsewhere, in the whole compass of the Old Testament.

To this deduction of the history of demonology throughout the books of the Old Testament, it may not be amiss to subjoin what occurs in the book of *Tobit*, relating to this subject; as this will shew the sense of the *Israelitish* church in his time; which was that of the *Assyrian* captivity of the ten tribes, when he was carried captive among them.

In this book we read of *Asmodeus*, the evil spirit, who had killed seven men successively, betrothed unto one woman, before *on Scripture Demonology.* 299

fore the confummation of their marriage with her *—And of *Raphael, one of the seven holy angels, which present the prayers of the saints, and which go in and out, before the glory of the Holy One* †. He was sent to bind *Asmodeus*, the evil spirit, and to chase him away, by a preparation of the heart and liver of a fish ‡. And the evil spirit accordingly fled unto the utmost parts of *Egypt*; and the angel bound him §.

This book is apocryphal, and every one is at liberty to believe as he pleases concerning this account of *Raphael* and *Asmodeus*. The driving of the evil spirit away with the smoke of the burnt heart and liver of a fish looks like a charm: But the doctrine, on account of which the story is mentioned, is agreeable to that of the *Jewish* church, in the preceding ages.

This book contains the memoirs of *Tobit* and his family, and is generally looked upon, by both *Jews* and Christians, as genuine history: And as such it contains an early account of obsessions and mischiefs done by evil spirits. Nor is this particular

* Tobit iii. 8. † Ch. xii. 15.
‡ Ch. vi. 7. 16. 17. § Ch. viii. 3.

relation

relation so incredible, if it be considered, that the most unlikely means have had virtue given them for particular purposes, which they were appointed for.

The waters of *Jordan* were impregnated with an efficacy for the cure of a leprosy, preferably to all others, in a particular case; though not, that we know of, for the cure of leprosies in general. And our Saviour's use of clay for the cure of blindness, was as unsuitable in itself, as the gall of the fish was for the cure of *Tobit's* eyes. And why might not other parts of the same fish have been impregnated with virtue, for frightening away the evil spirit? *Paul's* handkerchief had no virtue in itself for any salutary purpose; though it answered many*. Certain rites were made use of in exorcisms, together with the invocation of the God of *Abraham*, *Isaac*, and *Jacob*: And the use of mere charms and incantations by impostors arose from some forms and rites, which had been found effectual.

The practice of exorcising devils, by the name of the God of *Abraham*, *Isaac*, and *Jacob*, was in use among the *Jews* long

---

* Acts xix. 12.

before

before our Saviour's time. *Josephus* informs us, it was as antient as *Solomon*, who, he says, " improved that wisdom and knowledge which God had given him, for the benefit of men, and to the confusion of the devils—having left behind him forms of exorcising in writing, so effectual against evil spirits, that they fled before them, never daring to return: Which way of remedy, says he, prevails much among our people to this day." And he subjoins, his having been an eye-witness himself of one *Eleazer*, a countryman of his, dispossessing people in the presence of the emperor *Vespasian* *.

As for the manner of performing these dispossessions, and the charms which were used for the purpose, they are certainly ridiculous enough; and were probably the inventions of some late exorcists, or impostors, wherewith the practice was debased; and of whose juggling tricks they favour more than of the wisdom of *Solomon*; and perhaps were suggested by evil spirits, to expose and defeat the real efficacy of the exorcisms. That the practice itself was sometimes attended with success, is attested by

* Jos. Antiq. lib. viii. cap. 2.

our Saviour himſelf. *By whom do your ſons caſt them out**? This paſſage from *Joſephus* ſhews, that the notion of poſſeſſions and diſpoſſeſſions had long prevailed among the *Jews*, before his time; and adds no ſmall confirmation to the truth and reality of thoſe recorded in the goſpels.

Having deduced the hiſtory of *demoniſm* through the books of the Old Teſtament, and ſuch evidences of it as are to be had among the *Jews*, previous and ſubſequent to the goſpel age; it will be unneceſſary to carry this deduction through the evangelical writings; as we have already ſeen at large, in the former part of this work, what is delivered there, relating to *demons* and evil ſpirits. But to complete this hiſtory, it will be requiſite juſt to point out ſuch paſſages in the other books of the New Teſtament, as do more eſpecially relate to it. To which I ſhall prefix only one paſſage out of the goſpels, before taken notice of; to connect the ſenſe of the *Jews*, both *before*, and *after* Chriſt, concerning poſſeſſions, by ſhewing what it was *in* his time. *Say we not well, that thou*

* Luke xi. 19.

art a Samaritan, and haſt a devil*? Now though the *Jews* were ready enough to calumniate the *Samaritans* upon all occaſions; yet they could not have had any handle for it in this reſpect, had not the *Samaritans* been infamous at that time, for being under the influence of evil ſpirits.

We have ſeen inſtances of poſſeſſions in the *Acts* of the Apoſtles. Here too we read of *Simon Magus*, bewitching people with his ſorceries †; concerning whoſe nefarious practices, and impious opinions we meet with a good deal in the firſt writers of the church. In this book we read of *Elymas*, a noted ſorcerer likewiſe ‡. In the epiſtles, we find frequent mention of the devil, and his works—of the fallen angels—of the Gentiles worſhiping, and ſacrificing to devils—of ſome in the latter times giving heed to ſeducing ſpirits, and doctrines of devils—of principalities and powers—of the rulers of the darkneſs of this world—of the prince of the power of the air, as the devil is called—and of ſpiritual wickedneſſes in high places. We read of wicked perſons

* John viii. 48. † Acts viii. 9.
‡ Acts xiii. 8.

being

being delivered unto *Satan*, for the destruction of the flesh—And of St. *Paul*, the apostle of Christ; who, notwithstanding the abundance of the *Revelations* vouchsafed him, and the great progress he had made towards perfection, yet was not exempt from his snares and devices; there being *given him a thorn in the flesh, the messenger of Satan to buffet him* *. We have already had occasion to observe many things that occur both in the *Epistles* and *Revelation*, concerning this worst of Beings; which therefore are passed over, or but just touched upon here—That he *goeth about like a roaring lion, seeking whom he may devour*—That the man of sin should be revealed—*whose coming should be after the working of Satan, with all power, and signs, and lying wonders; and with all deceiveableness of unrighteousness* †. We are so much warned and cautioned against him in the word of God, *that we are not ignorant of his devices* ‡. We have already had occasion to observe, that the devil is more than once mentioned in the *Revelation*, by his names, *Satan, The old serpent,*

---

* 2 Cor. xii. 7.   † 2 Thes. ii. 8, 9, 10.
‡ 2 Cor. ii. 11.

and *The great dragon ; which deceiveth the whole world.* He is there also called, *The king of the locusts ;* which *had tails like scorpions, with stings in them ;* wherewith they had power to do great hurt: And he is said to be the angel of the bottomless pit, whose name is *Abaddon,* and *Apolluon**. The dragon is said to be worshiped †. And the devils in general are mentioned, as having worship paid them ‡. The dragon and his angels, fought with *Michael* and his angels; but was vanquished, and cast out into the earth, and his angels with him; where he persecuted the woman, which brought forth the man child; whom he endeavoured to devour as soon as he was born §. From hence we learn, that he was the author of the ten general persecutions ‖. See these matters particularly explained, in six discourses on select parts of the Revelation, preached, among others, at *Boyle's* lectures **. Lastly, we are here informed, that the devil was, or is, to be bound for a thousand years; after the expiration of which, he is to be loosed out of his prison,

* Prov. ix. 11.   † Rev. xiii. 4.
‡ Ch. ix. 20.   § Ch. xii.
‖ Ch. xx.   ** By Dr. Worthington

for a little feason; and fuffered to go out to deceive the nations; which are in the four corners of the earth. But that he is at length to be caft into the lake of fire and brimftone, there to be tormented, with the beaft, and falfe prophet, day and night, for ever and ever *.

Upon a retrofpect of the whole, we find, that there is a Being, known by the name of the Devil, who is the author of all moral evil; whence all natural evils likewife originate: And who therefore is juftly to be reckoned the evil principle. He introduced evil firft into the world; and ever fince hath been the great fupport, promoter, and fomenter of it—That he hath a numerous and formidable band of other apoftate fpirits, called his angels; who, together with him, fell from their firft eftate, and are united in confederacy with him; working together in feducing and withdrawing mankind from their duty to, and dependance upon God; inftigating to, and promoting all manner of fin and wickednefs in the world; darkening and perverting the reafon and underftanding of men; corrupting their wills and

* Ch. xx.

affections,

affections, and destroying their souls—That God, who brings good out of evil, makes use of the Devil, and his angels, in the government of the world—That, for this end, he thinks fit sometimes to give him great power over the elements of air and fire, and other parts of nature; over the brute creation; and likewise over the persons of men; so far as to permit him to take possession of, and act in, their bodies—But that his power is under controul; and subject to certain laws of restraint, which he dares not transgress, nor can resist—That the consummate malignancy of this inveterate enemy of mankind is ever prompting him to do all the mischief, of all kinds, that he can, in the world; but that he is checked, and over-ruled, by the supreme power of his, and our Almighty Creator; who protects his poor creatures; and suffers them not to be tempted by him, any farther than they are able to bear—That the good are tempted, and harrassed by him; but that wicked men are too often led away captive by him at his will—That he is employed for judgment; for correction; and even for mercy in the end—for the gradual reformation of a corrupt and wicked world; as we have reason to hope; and that the evil, which, by his inftrumentality, is permitted to reign, and prevail in the world, will at length terminate in the univerfal good.

It hath been confidently afferted by unbelievers, as an inconteftible fact, that poffeffions were a kind of new *phænomena*, that had not appeared, or but rarely, before the gofpel age; and that only among the people of the *Jews*: And this the friends of revelation have been called upon to account for; which fome of them taking the fact for granted, have endeavoured to do. But from the above view we have feen, that this was no new thing; but that there were always inftances of what might be reckoned poffeffions; or of cafes, from which poffeffions might be inferred, more or lefs, in the preceding ages, all over the world; even from the infancy of it. The Devil's entrance into the body of the ferpent to tempt *Eve*, was an early proof of the poffibility of the thing, with regard to mankind.

That we know fo little of poffeffions in the fucceeding ages, is no more than what happens in common with our ignorance of other things; from the want of the hiftory

both

both of nature and religion, in those times. We have no kind of history of the first ages of the world; but what we have in the bible; and that is very short. The rulers of darkness undoubtedly had great sway in those times of ignorance; which it was their policy to keep men in; and then the kingdom of darkness was at its greatest height, and spread most universally.

As the Devil, and his angels, were so busy among the people of God, we can conclude no less, than that they were much more so, among all the other nations of the world; who did not bear so near a relation to him; and whom he had not taken so immediately under his protection. How the *Egyptians*, for instance, dealt in inchantments, magick, and sorcery—what proficients they were in these diabolical arts; and of course, how much they were under the power and influence of the author of them; we may judge from what we have seen above.

From the king of *Israel*'s sending to consult *Baal-zebub*, the god of *Ekron**, it appears, that this was a famous heathen

* 2 Kings i. 2.

oracle.

oracle. And *Baal-zebub*, we are informed in the gospel, was the Devil. All the heathen oracles, which all idolatrous nations abounded with, before the gospel age, were dictated by him, through his priests, or more commonly his priestesses; which were possessed by him for that purpose.

Celsus recounts a good number of them, the *Pythian*; the *Dodonean*; the *Clarian*; the *Branchidian*; the *Ammonian*; and other oracles, says he, *innumerable* *.

Magick, and sorcery, were practised without reserve; and made part of the religion of all idolatrous nations: And it was upon the credit of these arts, that it was supported. And from hence, and from the testimony of many heathen writers, it appears, that possessions must have abounded more before the time of Christ, than is generally imagined.

The author of the Essay on Demoniacks hath furnished us with many authorities to this purpose. "Demonology, he observes, composed a very eminent part of the *Pythagorean* and *Platonick* philosophy:" And this, with possessions, and magick, says he,

---

* Origen contra Celsum, lib. vii. init.

seem

seem to have composed the common creed of all men, except the followers of *Democritus.* " And he further justly observes, that the established theology of the heathen world, from its first rise, to its final overthrow, rested upon the basis of demonism. And, as he adds, scarce was there a single oracle delivered, but by a person said to be possessed *."

" It appears, says he elsewhere, from the earliest writers, that *demoniacks* were thought to have *demons within them in person.*" For which he produces authorities from antient poets, historians, and philosophers; " which, with a thousand others, says he, serve to shew, that the general idea, which the antients entertained of demoniacks, was, that of persons, whose symptoms were ascribed to the real presence, and *residence* of *demons* in the human body †". And those few, who were of a different opinion, nay even those who wrote against this persuasion, bear testimony by their very writings, to the general notion of the reality of those posses-

---

* Essay on Demonology, P. 135, 6, 7.
† P. 71, note.

fions: And how that notion could obtain, and so much prevail, I cannot account for otherwise, than from its having been founded in truth.

To the instances which he hath given, the following may be added. *Homer* imputes a painful and wasteful distemper, under which a man had long languished, to a hateful *demon**. *Aretæus* relates, that some believed the epilepsy was called a *sacred disease*, from the supposition, that some *demon* had taken possession of the man that was seized with it †.

It appears from *Virgil's* description of the *Sibyl*, that she laboured under all the symptoms of possession ‡. *Euripides* expresses himself in such a manner, as if he supposed a number of *demons* might enter a man at one, and the same time §. The same notion occurs in *Plautus*. Hence *Amphitruo* says

* ———Εν νυσῳ κειται κρατερ' αλγεα πασχων.
Δηρον τηκομενος, ϛυϛερος δε οἱ εχραε δαιμων. Odyſ. v. 396.

† Δαιμονος δοξης ες τον ανθρωπον εισοδȣ.

‡ At Phœbi nondum patiens, immanis in antro
Bacchatur vates, magnum si pectore possit
Excussisse Deum ——— Æneis vi. 77.

§ Ὁταν γαρ ὁ Θεος εις το σωμ' ελθη πολυς.
Eurip. Bacch. v. 300.

of *Alcmena*, that she was *larvarum plena*—full of those mischievous spirits, the *Larvæ*; who were supposed to cause madness, and to inflict other disorders upon mankind *. Agreeably hereto, *Porphyry* acknowledges, as observed above, that both the houses, and bodies of some men were *full* of *demons* †.

These instances, with the foregoing observations, are sufficient to convince us, that the antient heathens, in ages preceding the gospel, had imbibed the notion of possessions; and that it was grown familiar among them.

But this is not all. They had a notion, not only of single possessions: But we see they were impressed with the persuasion of complicated ones likewise—of many demons possessing a man, in conjunction with each other. But the possibility of this, or of any such thing, could never have entered their thoughts, had they not seen some very strong and violent possessions, attended with a variety of strange symptoms, to convince them of the reality of it. These are introduced as matters of ordinary occurrence.

* Plaut. Amphitruo, Act ii. scene 2.
† See page 57.

There could be nothing new therefore, or ſtrange in them, at the time of the goſpel. Accordingly we do not find that theſe complicated caſes, any more than others, produced any wonder, or doubt among thoſe who were preſent, when they appeared before Chriſt; or that the reality of them was ever queſtioned, or caviled at by his enemies. Much leſs reaſon therefore, or colour have any at this time, for treating them with all that ſcorn and ridicule, which hath been caſt upon them *.

To proceed, as the worſhip of all nations, one only excepted, before the coming of Chriſt, was idolatrous; and poſſeſſions were incorporated with it; this gained them a general eſtabliſhment; and every heathen oracle was, of courſe, delivered by a ſettled and continued ſucceſſion of poſſeſſed perſons. Many heathen authors mention the exiſtence of demoniacks among them, excluſively of any relation they had to their oracles, of which we have ſeen ſome inſtances. And hence the frequency of them among the heathens is ſufficiently evinced; and likewiſe their having got to a

---

* See Eſſay on Demoniacks, p. 4, note from *Rouſſeau*.

greater

greater head in all heathen nations, than they could have had among the *Jews*; as their religion did not admit of any of the like oracles. But neither were *they* without an oracle to consult, on publick and emergent occasions; the appointment of which was most probably intended to counteract those heathen ones*: I mean the oracle of *Urim* and *Thummim*; which the high priest was to carry in his breast-plate. These names signified *light* and *perfection*, and denoted the clearness and perfection, which these oracular answers always carried; which were not like the heathen oracles, obscure, enigmatical and ambiguous; but always clear and manifest; never falling short of perfection, either of fulness in the answer, or certainty in the truth of them †.

The antient heathen nations, who *knew not God*; and *did not like to retain him in their knowledge,* when revealed to them, easily *fell into the snare of the Devil*; and *were taken captive by him at his will.* This

---

* Vide Spencer de leg. Hebræorum, lib. iii. differt. vii. cap. i. p. 854.
† Prid. Conn. part i. book iii.

might

might juftly be called his *hour, and the power of darkneſs.* He had had a long reign, and continued in undifturbed poffeffion of his kingdom; and it undoubtedly was his policy to maintain his poffeffion, with as little interruption, and as quietly, as poffible. He did not then perhaps plague men fo much; but ufed arts of foothing them under his bondage. It was not the bufinefs of this fubtle adverfary to vaunt of his power, and blaze it abroad; but to keep it as covertly as he could; and to infinuate himfelf, by ftealth into the bodies of men; and to lurk within them, as unobferved as might be; whereby his reign became the more abfolute and univerfal; the lefs fufpected, and therefore the lefs withftood.

Hence poffeffions were not fo much known, or taken notice of: The very commonnefs of them made them to be the lefs regarded; and the lefs recorded in hiftory. And as far as they were known, and obferved to prevail, the poor wretches, who fuffered by them, had in general no remedy; and therefore found it in vain to complain; but were obliged to languifh under their mifery, and bear it as well as they could.

This is the moft favourable view, in which

which the demoniacks of those times can be taken. But this was far from being always the case.

We have seen some heathen testimonies of possessions, in which the poor patients suffered terribly: And we meet with descriptions of their cases; which are very similar to those of the gospel.

Porphyry relates, " that some souls had demons at all times adhering to them, by which they were so overcome, as to be unmercifully racked and tortured by them *." And particularly we are informed upon the authority of *Plato*, and a heathen poet, that such as were possessed by a spirit of divination, and delivered oracles, bought that priviledge very dearly. For that they were distracted, and raved like madmen; not knowing themselves what they said; and that they were tossed and torn to that degree, as not to be able to bear the fury of the *demon*; and were obliged to beg a release from him in a prescribed form of words †.

But however poor mortals, who were under the dominion of evil spirits, were

---

* Euseb. præp. evang. lib. iv. cap. 22.
† Chrysost. op. tom iii. orat. 29 in 1 Cor.

deal

dealt with by them, when *the Son of righteousness arose with healing in his wings,* he brought these hidden works of darkness to light, and detected the workers of them.

No sooner was his power over evil spirits known, than there was a general resort to him from all quarters. *His fame was immediately spread abroad throughout all the region round about Galilee. And they brought unto him all that were possessed with devils; and he cast them out* *. The Devil was alarmed, when he saw our Saviour's design of destroying his kingdom, his power, and influence over mankind. This made him redouble his diligence, in arming himself against him; exerting all his might, and collecting all his forces to withstand him. He now saw all was at stake; and therefore mustered up his whole train of apostate angels; as far as he was permitted by the over-ruling power of his Almighty Creator, in defence of his kingdom of darkness; which he perceived was in imminent danger of being overthrown, by the great captain of our salvation. He strained all his powers. He summoned his forces together, in such

* Mark i. 28. 32.

numbers, and arranged them in such close order; that he contrived to croud a whole legion into the body of one man; in order to dispute the possession of this single person; being determined not to yield an inch of ground, that he could possibly keep.

When he found himself overpowered, his rage broke out into public expostulations—made him cry out aloud; and revenge himself in a most cruel manner, before whole multitudes, upon the poor demoniacks.

All this greatly increased the notoriety of possessions; from the commencement of Christ's ministry, beyond what had, or could have been, ever observed before; as there never had been such an emergency, for making them so conspicuous and observeable. To this we may add, that the great number of persons, who accompanied our Saviour, and the multitudes that every where crouded about him, when he performed these miracles upon the demoniacks, were all witnesses of them, and spread their fame far and wide.

From the whole therefore, I think we may venture to infer, that Mr. *Mede*, and others, believers and unbelievers, seem to have

have been too hasty in supposing the rareness of demoniacal possessions, before the times of the gospel; and that in those times, they abounded more in *Judea*, than in other countries; the contrary to which suppositions, we may, from the foregoing observations and instances, be induced to think was the real truth of the case.

The Devil's wrath is much provoked, and makes the effects of his malice and vengeance to be more felt, when he apprehends himself in danger. We find a caution to this purpose, on an occasion subsequent to these times. *Wo to the inhabitants of the earth, and of the sea! For the Devil is come down unto you, having great wrath; because he knoweth that he hath but a short time* *. And he undoubtedly fell upon the inhabitants of the world with great wrath likewise; when the seed of the woman, which was to bruise his head, appeared in the flesh; and consequently vented it more, as he perceived his reign was endangered, and the dissolution of his kingdom threatened.

If therefore there were more possessions in that age, than in the preceding ones;

* Rev. xii. 12.

and

on Scripture Demonology. 321

and more of them observed in the *Jewish* nation, than elsewhere, at that time; this sufficiently accounts for it: As the comparative silence of history concerning possessions; whether they were more, or less, in former times, and among other people, is accounted for from the foregoing considerations.

From the many accounts of demoniacks which we have in the gospels, we may collect, there were many kinds of devils, or demons, who possessed them—that there were different ranks, and orders of those wicked spirits; a distinction of qualities between them; and degrees of malignity and wickedness even among the devils themselves.

A difference of rank and order between them may possibly have been observed, in the use of the different names of Δαιμων and Δαιμονιον. And the latter being the diminutive of the former, may be designed to signify an evil spirit of an inferior rank. All the three evangelists, who record the case of the man, who had a legion of devils, make use of the word Δαιμων. St. Luke uses Δαιμονιον likewise. And it is this latter term which is used in all other possessions, excepting that of *Judas*; in which the terms made use of are, Σατανας and Διαβολος. That there were degrees of wickedness and malignity among them, we may infer from what is said of an evil spirit cast out of a man, and returning with seven other spirits *more wicked* than himself.

When we read, *This* KIND *goeth not out but by prayer and fasting*, we learn, not only, that there are several kinds of wicked spirits; but that there are some particularly obstinate, and more difficult to be expelled, than others. There were *deaf* and *dumb* spirits. These not only caused deafness and dumbness in those they possessed: But as they are often denominated deaf and dumb themselves; this indicates their having some qualities analogous to those disorders. They might be particularly sullen, producing the like temper in the demoniacks. And they might be struck dumb at the presence of our Saviour, to pre-signify the approaching dumbness of all the heathen oracles; which were soon to be everywhere silenced, at the preaching of the gospel. They certainly would not be thus particularly characterized, without some particular meaning.

We

We may recollect, that many of those that are mentioned in the gospel, are called foul, and unclean spirits.

They might be reckoned such on several accounts. First, on account of the impure and filthy thoughts which they suggested, and the sins of uncleanness, to which they instigated, and tempted mankind. Secondly, on account of their delighting in the fat and blood, and steam, and entrails of the beasts offered in sacrifice to them, as *Tertullian* observes*, upon the best authority. For the word of God assures us, that the gods of the heathens actually *did eat the fat of their sacrifices, and drank the wine of their drink offerings* †. And hence St. *Paul* very properly reckons, that the partaking of their sacrifices, was partaking of *the table of devils*, and drinking of *the cup of devils* ‡. But a heathen writer, who was much attached to *demons*, goes still farther; and says, that their chief delight was in blood, and impurities; and that they entered the bodies of those that feasted upon their sacrifices, that they might have a continued,

---
* Tert. Apologeticus, p. 23.
† Deut. xxxii. 38.
‡ 1 Cor. x. 21.

and full enjoyment of them *. But thirdly, they are called foul and unclean spirits likewise, from the parts of the human body, which they entered, and occupied. "This wicked and unclean spirit, says an antient writer, that inhabits a man's belly, as a serpent his hole in the earth; and being unclean, is fit to dwell in that place, which is the receptacle of ordure, they appositely call ventriloquists †." The person in whom he spake did not open his mouth. This spirit was therefore most commonly called Εγγαςριμυθος ‡: and sometimes, Εγγαςριμαντις, Στερνομαντις, and Εντερομαντις, a diviner from the belly, the breast, and the entrails. This was the אוב of the Old Testament, above taken notice of. Sometimes the voice seemed to proceed from under the arms.

* Μαλιςα δε αἱμαῖι χαιρεσι (Δαιμονες) και ταις ακαθαρσιαις· και απολαυουσι τῶων εισδυνονῖες τοις χρωμενοις.

Euseb. præp. evang. lib. iv. cap. 23. ex Porphyrio.

† Το εμφωλευον τη ανθρωπινη γαςρι πονηρον, και αξιον την κοπροδοχον οικειν ακαθαρῖον πνευμα, λιαν εμφερως προσοιομαχασιν Εγγαςριμυθον.

Ham. in Act. xvi. not. b. ex Photio.

‡ There is a peculiar propriety in the term Εγγαςριμυθος; which signifies, not only a ventriloquist; but likewise a fallacious one. For in the proper meaning of the word, Μυθος is a Fable. And therefore is particularly applicable to the lying oracles of the heathens.

Origen

Origen describes the priestess of the famous oracle of *Pythian Apollo*, and the manner of her receiving the spirit, in words which may be seen below; but which are so obscene, that I must excuse myself from translating them, that I may not offend the delicacy of the English reader—" Therefore, as he infers, pray consider, whether the uncleanness of this spirit be not fully evinced from hence? And this, as he goes on, is not what hath happened only once, or twice, which perhaps might be tolerated; but constantly, whenever the *Pythoness* is thought to foretell future events *."

Well therefore on this, and the former accounts, might some spirits be denominated foul and unclean in the gospel.

The author of the essay on demoniacks seems to have a great tenderness for the moral character of these spirits; and is loath to allow they were either *evil*, or *unclean* †. But enough surely hath been said, to evince the real propriety of both the one and the other of these epithets.

---

* Ἰϛορηται τοινυν περι της Πυθιας,—ὁτι περικαθεζομενη το της Κασαλιας ϛομιον, ἡ τȣ Απολλωνος προφητις δεχεται πνευμα δια των γυναικειων κολπων—δια τȣων, ὁ ὡς ϛεμις εν τῳ σωφρονι, (και) ανθρωπῳ βλεπειν, απȣ λεγεται (q. λεγεσθαι). ἡ και ἁπτεσθαι. Origen contra Celſ. lib. vii. p. 333.

† P. 61.

It is not for nothing that thefe accurfed fpirits are thus particularly characterized, and have thefe different denominations affixed to them. They feem to point out their fpecifick natures, and ill qualities, as well as their fpecial talents for infufing the like vicious qualities into men. Thus we read of a fpirit that lufteth unto envy; a fpirit of error; a fpirit of Antichrift; a fpirit of jealoufy; a fpirit of whoredoms; and a perverfe fpirit; as we read likewife of many good fpirits.

Like wicked men, who have their particular vicious habits, and propenfities; one fin reigning more in one man; and another in another; and fome being univerfal finners: And as fuch make it their bufinefs to feduce others; and not only *do things worthy of death themfelves, but take pleafure in thofe that do them*: So thofe wicked fpirits feem to have their predominant vices too; fome vices being more deeply implanted in fome of them, and others, in others: Which it is their fpecial province to tempt men to, in order to affimilate them, as much as may be, to themfelves: Whilft others again are more univerfally wicked; and have a genius, if I may be allowed the expreffion, for undertaking

taking any mifchief; and inftigating to any vice. And accordingly they are all inceffantly employed in projecting and working the deftruction of mankind, in one fhape or other.

This is as much as I have been able to extract concerning the devil, and his angels, out of the holy fcriptures; in which alone any certain information about them is to be found. It is alledged, that the light of nature difcovers not the exiftence of fallen angels*. And this is readily allowed. We may ranfack all the ftores of human learning; but fhall never be able to find any light from them into the world of fpirits, that can be depended upon. The demonology of the antient heathens, and of their philofophers, was grounded, partly upon tradition, derived from the fall; partly upon their own too fatal experience, and obfervation, concerning the intercourfe, which fome invifible beings muft have had with mankind; and partly, I doubt not, they were mifled by the *ignis fatuus* of the *demons* themfelves, to judge concerning them otherwife than they really were in themfelves.

* Effay on Demoniacks, p. 151.

What is most considerable in any heathen writings in this respect, is the doctrine of the two principles; the one good, the other evil; the former being represented by light, the latter by darkness—That these two principles were constantly contending with each other; but that the good principle shall at last prevail, and triumph over the evil one—That the one is called Θεος, God; and the other Δαιμων, Devil, as we translate.

This opinion was so antient, that *Plutarch* did not know whom to ascribe it to. The founder of it is generally supposed to have been *Zoroaster*, though he ought rather to be esteemed its reformer. The good principle he called *Oromasdes*; the evil one, *Arimanius*. Now *Zoroaster* is, upon good grounds, supposed to have been a *Jew.* He reformed the Magian religion, upon a Jewish platform; and wrote a book conformable to the scripture doctrines. He taught, that under the Supreme Being, there was an angel of light, and an angel of darkness, in perpetual struggle with each other, and that this contest shall continue to the end of the world; when there shall be a general judgment. After which th angels

angels of darkness shall be sent to a world of their own; where they shall suffer in everlasting darkness, the punishment of their evil deeds.

Hence it is evident, that this impostor was not unacquainted with the revolt of the fallen angels, and the entrance of evil into the world that way. And hence it appears, that the best notions, which the heathens had of evil spirits, were drawn from the Jewish scriptures; and those notions much corrupted *.

Hence it is plain likewise, that the holy scriptures are the only source we have to draw from in this respect. We have no *data* of our own to proceed upon, in researches of this kind. The nature of these invisible Beings, like themselves, is too subtle for our metaphysicks to attain any knowledge of. Every man however ought to have as much knowledge concerning his spiritual enemies, as is necessary to preserve him from their snares. And as this is to be had from the scripture alone; it must certainly be very pernicious to corrupt this sacred fountain,

---

* Plutarch de Iside et Osiride. Prid. Connex. part I. book iv.

and to pervert the sense of scripture relating to it. To represent these as impotent enemies, that have no power to hurt us, is making them to be no more than bug-bears to frighten children: And this, I am sorry to say it, is the tendency of the essay on demoniacks. The demonology of which lies in a very narrow compass.

The declared purport of it is, to argue us out of the reality of possessions, and to persuade us, that they are only imaginary, and the notion superstitious—That possessing demons were esteemed to be only departed souls; and these are reduced to non-entities—That neither the Devil, nor his angels had any concern in possessions at all; and that the Devil is never mentioned in scripture in any connection with this subject *: The contrary to which I flatter myself, is in the foregoing sheets made very evident. Other positions of the same tendency maintained by this author are—" That it is absurd and dangerous to allow, that men are in the power of superior malevolent spirits †."— " That whoever the heathen demons, or deities were, whether human or angelick

* Essay, p. 385. † Ibid. p. 168.

spirits,

spirits, they are all, without exception, branded in scripture, as being utterly void of all power, to do either good, or evil to mankind *"—" That the Devil was not really, and personally present with Christ, in his temptation; and could act no part in that whole transaction †;" notwithstanding what the gospel informs us to the contrary— " That there is but *one* Devil;" which is observed more than once ‡: And I do not find, that he is supposed to be a real tempter at all; though he is expressly so called in the word of God; or allowed to concern himself with mankind in any respect. But that he is a kind of solitary, insignificant, inactive Being, that seems only to fill up a blank in the creation. How just a representation of him this is, appears from the whole and every part of what hath been here said concerning him.

A rhetorical passage out of *Tertullian* is indeed quoted, which gives him a kind of ubiquity §; in common with angels, and

* Essay, p. 191.
† Enquiry into Christ's temptation in the wilderness, p. 85.
‡ P. 207, 305. of the Essay on Demoniacks.
§ Essay, p. 263. Tert. Apologet. p. 22.

demons

demons in general: But for what purpose I know not, unless it be to insinuate, that by being supposed to be every where, he is no where.

This is the demonology of this author, which is not only contrary to the scripture account of it here laid down; but diametrically opposite likewise to the very letter, sense, and whole tenour of the scripture itself, from the one end of it to the other.

He hath made short work with the Devil, and his angels; and hath done more than all the exorcists put together ever pretended to. He hath laid the Devil, and all other evil spirits; banished them out of the world; and in a manner destroyed their very existence. And if this be the case, we are absolutely delivered from one third part of our spiritual enemies; and those the most dangerous of any.

And since he is gone so far, I do not see why he might not proceed one step farther, to complete this goodly system. For as he seems to be persuaded, that *Beelzebub*, and all other *demons*, are non-entities; why should he boggle at allowing the Devil to be the self-same Being with *Beelzebub*, when there is sufficient proof of it; and more than

than sufficient to convince a well-inclined mind? And then, why not annihilate him likewise?

This would be doing acceptable service to libertines, free-thinkers, and all the infidel tribe; in ridding them of so troublesome a guest, as he otherwise would sometimes be, and of all gloomy apprehensions concerning him.

But let them be assured, that the Devil is not a name, or word, contrived to scare and affright timorous people with. He is a real Being, though generally invisible to our fleshly eyes; but not therefore the less dangerous enemy. If he were to appear in his own nakedness and deformity; that would counteract his attempts upon us, and be alone sufficient to make us shun him, and bless ourselves from him—But uncloathed and unbodied natures may converse with us by secret illapses, while we are not aware of them. And as there is a good spirit, conversant in the world; inviting and influencing mankind to virtue and holiness: So is there an evil spirit, who is ever busying himself in tempting them to sin and vice, and drawing them into a resemblance to himself. For the Devil, and his angels did

not

not fall from Heaven so much, by a local descent, as by a mental apostacy from, and dissimilitude of God. They were indeed cast down into a local hell likewise; but we have seen, they are not all, nor at all times, strictly confined there: And we have too good proofs of their enlargement and liberty, to need the descending thither to seek them, or to use any magical charms to fetch them up from thence *. *Satan* is perpetually ranging and roving about the world. This we have his own word for. He repeatedly confessed to his Maker, that he came *from going to and fro in the earth, and from walking up and down in it* †. And the Apostle assures us, that our *adversary the Devil, as a roaring lion, walketh about, seeking whom he may devour* ‡. And he uses this as an argument of sobriety and vigilance against him.

But how opposite to the word of God, and to the design of our holy religion; and how pernicious to the souls of men is it, to broach any opinions, or suggest any insinuations, of a contrary tendency? This is putting us off our guard, and lulling us asleep,

---

* See Smith's Select Discourses, p. 47.
† Job i. 7.   ‡ 1 Pet. v. 8.

when the enemy is in our quarters; besetting us on every side; and playing all his artillery against us. It is acting the part of a confederate. It is fighting under his banner; and betraying our fellow-creatures, and ourselves too, it is to be feared, into his snares.

And this I must own appears to me to be the plain tendency of the unsettling of our faith in our Lord's temptation; and of that relating to diabolical possessions. If the scripture had been silent about Christ's temptation; there had been no foundation for our faith in it. But this is mentioned as a fact by three evangelists; and very particularly and circumstantially recorded by two of them; and we are elsewhere assured by the word of God, that he was *in all things tempted like unto ourselves*: And yet the reality of this fact is disputed. And if any can be induced to think that Christ was not tempted at all; I do not see what should hinder them from flattering themselves; that neither are *they* obnoxious to temptations; whatever they are taught to the contrary.

So likewise, though the Devil and his angels never gave such palpable proofs of their intermeddling with mankind, in the

great

great affair of their falvation; and never exerted themfelves fo openly, in any other methods of mifchief, and deftruction, as in that of poffeffions; if notwithftanding men fuffer themfelves to be perfuaded, that there was nothing real in them; they will be tempted to laugh at the imperceptible affaults of their fpiritual enemies; and may be bantered out of the belief of their very exiftence.

Thus hath this man been tugging at the two main pillars, on which the fcripture doctrine concerning the exiftence of the Devil, or any other evil fpirits, refts: Which yet, I truft, will ftand. If he doth not mean totally to deftroy this doctrine, he fhould let us know, how thefe fupports of it may be fufficiently replaced; and what others equivalent to them, he thinks fit to leave us, for the foundation of our faith in this refpect.

If we begin to entertain flight notions of the deadly enemy of our fouls; and grow regardlefs of his power to hurt us; we expofe ourfelves an eafy prey to him, who hath manifold arts and ftratagems, for feducing unwary mortals, and drawing them into his fnares.

It

It behoves us therefore, as we tender our own safety, to watch and pray ; and to *put on the whole armour of God, that we may be able to stand in the evil day*; and against the evil one. We should have our *senses exercised to discern both good and evil*: Then we shall not be *ignorant of his devices*, and as dreadful an enemy as he is, we need not be dismayed at him. For we are assured, that if we do but *resist him, he will flee from us*.

Hear the words of an antient christian, who speaks from his own experience. " This we can affirm, says he, from our own experience, that they who worship and serve God, through Jesus Christ, in a christian manner, living according to his gospel, and persevering in the use of fervent prayer night and day, are in no danger from any magical arts, or devils: For that *the angel of the Lord encampeth round about them, that fear him, and delivereth them* *."

In this age of the gospel, when the light of it, God be praised, is become so prevalent, that the powers of darkness can the less bear it; and are much checked and weakened, in their influence on the chris-

* Origen contra Celf. lib. vi. p. 302.

tian world; by its illumination of the understandings of men; and the general reformation, which it hath made in the lives of christians; we seldom, if ever, have any certain account of possessions, or obsessions. And hence it is, that many have been induced to think, there never were in reality any such. But we have still *rulers of darkness* to contend with: And there is a spirit that still *worketh in the children of disobedience*, more covertly, and subtily perhaps: But that affords us no grounds for supineness, and security.

The notion of witchcraft is now exploded; and the wisdom and humanity of our legislature is much to be commended, for the repeal of those laws that had been made against it; whereby I doubt not many innocent persons, in times past, suffered. Nor, I believe, are there any grounds for thinking, that a single guilty person hath escaped punishment by the repeal of them. And yet I will not take upon me to pronounce, that there never was any occasion for those laws, before they were made; and that none of all those seemingly well attested cases of witchcraft were real, though some of them were attended with very extraordinary,

traordinary, and otherwise unaccountable circumstances.

This is certain, that charms and sorceries were made use of in those times, for the discovery of witches: These were direct applications to infernal spirits; and it is not improbable, but that they might have struck in with them: And the word of God informs us, *That by sorceries all nations have been deceived**. The good riddance which in this age we have had of them, is one instance, among many others, of the benefit which we receive from the increasing light of the gospel.

Notwithstanding this, I do not see, that any man can pronounce, there are no such *phænomena*, as witchcraft, or possessions at present; much less, that there cannot be any such.

We have seen, what a learned man, who lived about two centuries ago, declared concerning the reality of several possessions, which he had been an eye-witness of †: And his testimony cannot be refused, especially by a person, that produces him, as a witness for another purpose ‡.

* Rev. xviii. 23.   † P. 208, above.
‡ Essay on Demoniacks, p. 53.

Other authors of good credit, who flourished about the same time, and later, affirm, that they themselves, among many others, had seen ventriloquists, and heard them speak out of their bellies, and other parts of their bodies.

"*Aug. Eugabinus* affirms, that he himself had seen such women, called *ventriloquæ* (which is the same with the Greek εγγαςριμυθοι), from whom, as they sat, a voice came out of their secret parts; and gave answers to enquiries. And *Cælius Rhodiginus* (lib. viii. Antiq. Lect. cap. 10.) saith, this is not to be entertained with laughter; for not only he saw such a woman; and heard a very small voice coming out of her belly; but innumerable other people, not only at *Rhodigium*; but in a manner through all *Italy*. Among whom there were many great persons, who had her stript naked, that they might be sure there was no fraud; to whom a voice answered unto such things as they enquired. *Hieron. Oleaster* also, upon Isaiah xxiv. 4, saith, he saw such a one at *Lisbon*; from under whose arm-holes, and other parts of her, a small voice was heard, which readily answered to whatever was asked [*]."

[*] Bishop Patrick's Comment. on Levit. xix. 31.

These

These are all grave writers, who lived not above two ages ago; and whose testimony has a right to be received by us, as it was by Bishop *Patrick*; who gives his sanction to it. And what hath been, may be again.

Leo Allatius likewise hath collected various instances of ventriloquists; which, as I know no reason for doubting about them, on the one hand, so I will not vouch for the authenticity of them, on the other *.

Evil

---

* *Leonis Allatii* de Engastrimytho Syntagma, cap. iv. This learned writer confirms the description given above, p. 317, of the violent paroxysms of fury, with which the *Pythonesses* were seized, and tortured, even almost unto death. Ibid.

He likewise describes their voice, as being not articulate, distinct, or clear; but slender, squeaking, and perplexed; that by its obscurity, the lies which it uttered might be the less discovered, cap. v. Agreeably to the account given in this *Appendix*, page 278. In the following chapters, he also considers at large, the celebrated question, whether *Samuel* appeared in person, when called up by the witch of *Endor*; or whether it was not some wicked *demon*, that assumed his likeness, and represented him. He gives us the opinion of *Origen*, and some other fathers, for the reality of his appearance. And likewise the opinion and arguments of *Eustathius*, with whom many other fathers, and antient writers of

Evil Beings have been supposed to take advantage of the indisposition of the body, to affect the imagination, and to disorder the brain; whereby madnesses, that are so common, may often have been caused. The ravings and distractions of *Pythonesses*, and others, that professed to foretell future events, by the suggestions of such spirits, are instances in proof of this point: And we know not how far such foreign powers may contribute to other madnesses: But that possession and madness are convertible terms, and that all demoniacal cases are to be resolved into madnesses, and epilepsies, and those only natural disorders, is a presumption without

great note, concur, in refutation of *Origen*, and support of the other side of the question. And concludes, that the opinion of *Eustathius* is the more probable, more consonant to truth, and to the authority of the fathers; and more agreeable to the text of holy scripture likewise. And I have the happiness of finding, that what I have advanced above, on this, as well as the foregoing heads, is agreeable to the sentiments of this learned man; and abundantly confirmed by him, out of the writings of the antients: Which I did not know, when I had these points under consideration: Otherwise I probably would have profited more by, and made a better use of his labours; which I now can only refer to.

any

any proof at all; and hath been shewn to be contrary to fact in many cases.

A good reasoner hath made it extremely probable, that all men are subject to impressions, which are of the same kind, in an inferior degree, with possessions; and that we are all visited with them, or liable to them, every night of our lives. Dreaming is a *phænomenon*, which many antients and moderns have attempted to account for: But none, I conceive, in so satisfactory a manner, as this writer. He observes, "that this appearance cannot be the effect of mechanism; but must proceed from some living, designing cause. Many of our dreams are so odd, and so much out of the sphere of a man's own knowledge, that they cannot be caused by his own imagination, or any of his own faculties.—That therefore they must be suggested to him, by some foreign spiritual Being, impressing the idea upon the sensory; by means of which, the soul, which is passive, hath it by communication; and that way becomes the percipient of it," in much the same manner, we may suppose, as one waking man perceives what is communicated to him by another. " And thus, says he, by easy steps we see, that *dreaming may degenerate into possession*; and that the cause, and nature of both is the same; differing only in degree. For dreaming is but *possession* in sleep; from which we are relieved again, when we awake; and external objects begin to solicit the perceptivity through the senses *."

" This notion of our dreams degenerating into a waking possession, he elsewhere tells us, is not entirely new; as we may see from those authors, which he quotes, who had written on this subject before him. Whatever way a man accounts for these two *phænomena*, he will readily give the same solution for both; there being such an affinity between them †."

Here we see, that the reality of these supernatural cases, which we read of in scripture, is countenanced by natural appearances; which constantly present themselves to us. Revelation, in these instances, hath the sanction of sound philosophy; and

---

* Essay on the Phænomenon of Dreaming, vol. ii. p. 131, of a treatise entitled, An Enquiry into the Nature of the Human Soul.

† Ibid. p. 150.

possessions are well illustrated, and confirmed by our very dreams.

Let it here however be considered, that though we are liable to the incursions of evil spirits; and some of our most frightful dreams are suggested by them; yet that their commission is limited—That they are licensed to go so far, and no farther—And that they cannot touch a hair of our head, without the divine permission. *God is about our path, and about our bed**. *And the angel of the Lord encampeth round about them, that fear him, and delivereth them* †. Let it be considered farther, that even our most terrifying dreams do not always proceed from malevolent spirits; and that we are not to conclude from that circumstance, that they are the authors of them. No dream, nor night-vision, could be more terrible, than that of *Eliphaz* in *Job*: And yet it was caused by a holy angel; as appears from the doctrine delivered by him, at the close of it.

Now a thing was secretly brought to me, and mine ear received a little thereof. In thoughts from the visions of the night, when

† Psalm cxxxix. 2.   † Psalm xxxiv. 7.

deep sleep falleth on men. Fear came upon me, and trembling; which made all my bones to shake.

Then a spirit passed before my eyes: The hair of my head stood up.

It stood still; but I could not discern the form thereof; An image was before mine eyes; there was silence, and I heard a voice saying,

Shall mortal man be more just than God? Shall a man be more pure than his maker *?*

That impressions may be made on our faculties in sleep by foreign powers, will admit of no doubt, if it be but recollected, that many instances occur in scripture of the interposition of angels, and even of God himself, in dreams, and night-visions †. *For God speaketh once, yea twice, yet man perceiveth it not.*

In a dream; in a vision of the night, when deep sleep falleth upon men; in slumberings upon the bed. Then he openeth the ears of men; and sealeth their instruction ‡.

---

* Job iv. 12. 17.
† See Gen. xx. 3. 6 —xxxi. 11. 24. Numb. xii. 6. 1 Kings, iii. 5. Matt. i. 20.—ii. 12.
‡ Job xxxiii. 14. 15. 16.

It

It is confonant to our notions of the goodnefs of the divine providence, and of God's care for his creatures; as well as to the exprefs words of fcripture, to believe; that as there are malignant and deftroying angels; fo there are good ones, who are appointed by him to be the guardians of good men efpecially; and, as we have feen, to prefide over empires and kingdoms; and to infpect, and adminifter the affairs of them*.

The antient heathens had the like perfuafion, however they came by it, that every man had his good *demon* appointed him, as foon as he was born into the world, to be the guide and guardian of his life †. And the *demon* of *Socrates* is a remarkable inftance, which greatly confirms the truth of it. His only reftraining him from evil, but never exciting him to good, is however an indication of what partial and imperfect helps the beft of men had, in a ftate of nature, for the prefervation of their virtue, by the

---

* Dan. x. 13. 21.—xii. i. Zech. i. 8.—vi. 1. 8.

† Απαντι Δαιμων ανδρι συμπραςατει ευθυς γενομενῳ, μιςαγωγος τȣ βιȣ αγαθος. Menander.

inftrumentality

instrumentality of spirits with such limited powers; in comparison with that plentiful effusion of preventing, restraining, strengthening, exciting, and all kinds of graces, vouchsafed by God's holy spirit to good men, under the gospel dispensation.

The young disciples of Christ have their *angels*, who are always observing *the face of* their heavenly *Father*, to know his pleasure concerning them *. *They that be with us are more than they that be with them.* This was *Elisha's* assured reflection, when he shewed his young man the mountain full of horses and chariots of fire, round about him, to protect him against the host of the *Syrians*; which encompassed the city, in order to seize, and carry him away †. God sent his angel to shut the mouths of the lions, that they could not hurt *Daniel* ‡. *He giveth his angels charge over us.* For are *they not all ministering spirits, sent forth to minister for them, who shall be heirs of salvation* § ?

* Matt. xviii. 10.   † 2 Kings, vi. 15.
‡ Dan. vi. 22.   § Heb. i. 14.

Everlasting God, who hast ordained and constituted the services of angels and men in a wonderful order: Mercifully grant, that as thy holy angels always do thee service in heaven; so by thy appointment, they may succour and defend us on earth, through Jesus Christ our Lord. Amen.

F I N I S.

ERRATA.

Page 49, l. 14, for *very ill one*, r. *very ill contrived one*.
    55, l. 1, for *deprecate*, r. *depreciate*.
    65. l. 19, for *appointed*, r. *anointed*.
    324, Add to the text at the bottom of the page, *And sometimes out of the earth.*

BOOKS *lately published*;

And sold by J. F. and C. RIVINGTON, in St. Paul's Church-yard; T. PAYNE, at the Meuse Gate; and B. WHITE, in Fleet-street.

AN Essay on Redemption, octavo, second Edition.

The Historical Sense of the Mosaick account of the Fall proved and vindicated.

Instructions concerning Confirmation.

A Disquisition concerning the Lord's Supper.

The Evidences of Christianity, deduced from facts, and the testimony of sense, throughout all ages of the church, to the present time. In a series of discourses, preached for the Lecture founded by the Hon. Robert Boyle, Esq. in the parish church of St. *James, Westminster*, in the years 1766, 1767, 1768. Wherein is shewn, that, upon the whole, this is not a decaying, but a growing evidence. Two volumes, 8vo. 12s. By William Worthington, D. D.

The Scripture Theory of the Earth, throughout all its Revolutions, and all the Periods of its Existence, from the Creation to the final Renovation of all things. Being a sequel to the above Essay on Redemption, and an illustration of the principles on which it is written. One vol. 6s.

Irenicum; or, the Importance of Unity in the Church of Christ considered; and applied towards the healing of our unhappy differences and divisions.

All by the above AUTHOR.

www.ingramcontent.com/pod-product-compliance
Lightning Source LLC
Chambersburg PA
CBHW030256240426
43673CB00040B/982